Contents

Introduction   4

Commentary   5

Contexts   52
What did Shakespeare write?   52
What did Shakespeare read?   55
What was Shakespeare's England like?   62
  Jacobean social structure   65
  Patriarchal authority in Jacobean England   66
  Childbirth   68
  Male friendships   69
  Religion, grace and redemption   69
  Theatre   71
  Time   73

Language   75
Imagery   76
Antithesis   79
Repetition   80
Lists   82
Verse and prose   83

Critical approaches   86
Traditional criticism   86
Modern criticism   95
  Political criticism   96
  Feminist criticism   99
  Performance criticism   102
  Psychoanalytic criticism   104
  Postmodern criticism   105

Organising your responses   108
Writing about an extract   108
Writing an essay   114
Writing about character   118

Resources   126
Books   126
Films   128
Audio books   128
The Winter's Tale on the Web   128

Introduction

'A sad tale's best for winter' says the young prince Mamillius to his mother. His remark is full of prophetic irony; he is the first to be sacrificed to Leontes' paranoiac jealousy. Jealousy is the driving force of the first part of the play and it is all-consuming. Love is the driving force of the second part, with the constancy of Florizel and Perdita overcoming a father's anger and the obstacles of social class.

Shakespeare structures the two parts of *The Winter's Tale* around the figure of Time, who speaks of the 16 years' 'wide gap of time', of Leontes' grief and of the progress of Perdita in the home of the kindly Shepherd. It is a play which is full of oppositions: court versus country, nature versus art, winter versus spring, birth versus death, men versus women. In the tragic first three acts, the over-heated emotional scenes in Sicilia contrast with the freshness and piety of Cleomenes and Dion's description of Delphos. In Bohemia, the idealised pastoral world is set against the bawdy realism of Autolycus, and Mopsa and Dorcas.

The Winter's Tale can also be interpreted as resonant with parallels and echoes. Just as Leontes is king in Sicilia, Perdita is queen of the sheep-shearing feast; the sudden jealousy of Leontes is mirrored by the abrupt rage of Polixenes; Camillo is the trusted adviser of both Leontes and of Polixenes; Camillo and Paulina each act as directors of part of the action; Hermione is the focus of the trial and of the statue scene. The tragic and the comic parts of the play are also linked by imagery, language and wordplay.

The play that begins with potential tragedy ends with repentance and renewal, and the fulfilment of the oracle. The theatrically symbolic statue scene brings together mother and daughter, restores Hermione to the repentant Leontes, reunites Leontes and Polixenes and unites Camillo and Paulina.

The Winter's Tale is one of the last plays that Shakespeare wrote. It has all the attributes of these 'late' plays; intricate language patterns, contrasts and reflections, vivid imagery, loss and restoration, miracles and wonder and a tragi-comic structure. From Robert Greene's prose story *Pandosto*, which ends with the suicide of the repentant king, Shakespeare crafts a moving play of forgiveness and redemption.

Commentary

Act 1 Scene 1

At the beginning of *The Winter's Tale* Shakespeare uses a technique that he has used several times before, that of having minor characters introduce both the major characters and some of the themes of the play. In this play, Camillo of Sicilia and Archidamus of Bohemia are discussing the affairs of their masters: Leontes, King of Sicilia, and Polixenes, King of Bohemia. The audience learns that Polixenes has been on a visit to his childhood friend, Leontes, and that there is a planned return visit at some unspecified time in the future. They also discuss the benefits conferred by Mamillius, Leontes' young son.

Michael Billington, the theatre critic, calls the first sentence of the play 'Shakespeare's worst opening', and it is true that the hesitation and confusion does not have the abrupt dramatic quality of the first words of *Hamlet* or *Macbeth*. However, the opening gives the audience a very powerful impression of the uncertainty felt by the courtiers. Why should Archidamus feel it necessary to be so worried about the hospitality that Bohemia can offer Sicilia in return? Is there perhaps a suggestion that Sicilia is a more sophisticated society? The extent of his care seems disturbing. Through Archidamus' words, 'We will give you sleepy drinks, that your senses, unintelligent of our insufficience, may, though they cannot praise us, as little accuse us', and also in the fragmented phrasing of the speech, Shakespeare suggests a deep-seated anxiety. Archidamus struggles to find a way of expressing himself: 'I know not what to say'. Shakespeare could be suggesting that there is a marked difference between the two courts, with Sicilia more sophisticated and wealthy, an interpretation that could be supported by the only evidence of Bohemian life in the play in Act 4. On the other hand, Shakespeare may be establishing a picture of a formal, polite court life that will be contrasted with the informal scenes of country life in Act 4.

Camillo is reassuring. He refers to the kings' early friendship and the common practice during the Renaissance of having young people 'trained' for their future in the household of another lord. He uses natural imagery to emphasise their friendship. The imagery of the tree reflects the close relationship between the two kings in their boyhood, but it is also potentially ambiguous: 'rooted' suggests something which is firm and secure, and though 'branch' could mean the growth and flourishing of the friendship, 'branch' also suggests division. Even his assertion that they 'shook hands, as over a vast; and embraced as it were from the ends of opposed winds' stresses the distance between them as much as their friendship. Even the absolute conviction of Archidamus' response paradoxically gives a warning of potential trouble:

> I think there is not in the world either malice or matter
> to alter it.   *(lines 26–7)*

The tone of the conversation becomes more cheerful when the 'young prince' Mamillius is mentioned. The imagery that Camillo uses to describe him focuses on his powers to regenerate: 'makes old hearts fresh'. This is something on which both men can agree and even joke.

In this first scene Shakespeare gives important information to the audience and also establishes several of the major themes of the play. The dramatic purpose of this short scene seems to be to give the impression that there is lifelong deep 'rooted' affection between Polixenes and Leontes, and that Mamillius is a child of 'greatest promise'. Close analysis suggests that, though the language of Scene 1 is uniformly positive, there is an underlying sense of unease conveyed by the emphasis on the firmness of the friendship between the two kings.

Act 1 Scene 2

Polixenes is taking leave of his hosts, Leontes and Hermione, though at first the dialogue is only between him and Leontes. His stay has been quite a long one and the precise time, nine months, becomes more significant as the scene progresses. His expression of gratitude for Leontes' hospitality echoes Archidamus' elaborate speeches in the previous scene as he says he could spend nine further months in thanking Leontes and still be indebted for 'perpetuity'. Their close friendship is emphasised by the use of the word 'brother'. Polixenes is quite firm about wishing to return to his home: he is worried about possible problems caused by his long absence, and he has no wish to outstay his welcome.

Throughout this exchange Leontes and Polixenes share lines of verse. Conventionally this would suggest little or no pause between the speeches (see page 85) and so a rapid exchange of dialogue in the first 19 lines. The pace changes at line 20 with Polixenes' explanation of his feelings. He seems to have been made to feel uncomfortable by the repeated insistence on his remaining in Sicilia. The break in the lines and repetition reinforce his unease:

> Press me not, beseech you, so.
> There is no tongue that moves, none, none i'th'world
> So soon as yours could win me.   *(lines 19–21)*

By this time the audience possibly feels that Polixenes has made a good case for leaving, his 'affairs / Do even drag' him home. Nine months is a long time to leave a country without a ruler.

Having established the tension between the two men, Shakespeare introduces the third key figure, Hermione. Leontes asks his wife to join him in persuading Polixenes. His question, 'Tongue-tied, our queen?', seems to release her verbal power. Her language is forceful, and the only excuse she will accept as valid is his desire to see his son, a reason not offered by Polixenes who has concentrated on his fears about what may be happening to his 'affairs' at home. This is the first time the audience has heard mention of Polixenes' son and it may be that Shakespeare is giving an echo of the virtues and regenerative power ascribed to Leontes' son, Mamillius.

Hermione insists that Polixenes should stay at least one more week. In return she will allow Leontes to stay a whole month longer than arranged when he pays the return visit to Bohemia (the prospect of which has worried Archidamus so much). Her promise is made in spite of the fact that she claims to love Leontes no less than any lady could love her lord ('not a jar o'th'clock behind').

Her repeated insistence on his staying, playing with Polixenes' own word 'verily', makes it impossible for Polixenes to maintain his good manners and still refuse. She pushes the discourse of hospitality to its limits: 'My prisoner, or my guest?' Once he has conceded defeat, Hermione changes the subject abruptly, questioning Polixenes about the companionship of the two kings when they were boys. Shakespeare has already established in Scene 1 that they were 'trained together'. Hermione's language prompts Polixenes to reveal their mischievous behaviour ('tricks') when they were children. Polixenes idealises their childhood:

> We were, fair queen,
> Two lads that thought there was no more behind
> But such a day tomorrow as today,
> And to be boy eternal.   *(lines 62–5)*

When Hermione won't leave the idea of their misbehaviour and persists in her questions, Polixenes uses even more striking imagery to refute her. He speaks of the boys as 'twinned lambs', living entirely innocent lives. He goes so far as to claim that, if their lives had never changed, they would have been able to claim forgiveness even from Original Sin. In the Christian tradition, the doctrine of Original Sin asserts that all men and women are born sinful because of the Fall of Adam and Eve. Hermione's return to teasing with 'By this we gather / You have tripped since' is rather shocking because of the strong contrast between her words and Polixenes' exaggerated claims. He speaks in measured verse with almost all the punctuation mid-line to make the lines more resonant. His words are very powerful, evoking a sense of profound innocence which is abruptly broken by Hermione's 'tripped' with its slight suggestion of a fall from grace.

Polixenes retains his elevated tone calling Hermione 'most sacred lady'. He also implies that his and Leontes' mature sins are concerned with sexuality, as in their 'unfledged days' neither he nor Leontes had met their wives. Not surprisingly, Hermione wonders whether she is being compared to the devil. Her words continue to concentrate on sexual wrongdoing: 'offences . . . sinned . . . fault . . . slipped'.

Leontes returns to ask 'Is he won yet?' and here any director or editor of the play has decisions to make. When did Leontes leave Polixenes and Hermione to talk alone? More importantly, when does he return? Many editors guess that he would leave somewhere between line 37 and line 43. Clearly he must be back by line 86. Some editors even print appropriate stage directions, but these are not Shakespeare's and it makes an interesting exercise to try the effect of alternatives. The actor playing Leontes also has a decision to make about the delivery of the line 'At my request he would not.' Is this the turning point in Leontes' mood? Is he first made angry because his best friend has conceded to his wife and not to him?

He immediately congratulates Hermione on her powers of persuasion: 'thou never spok'st / To better purpose'. Hermione's response (lines 90–101) is full of questions, asking her husband to tell her about the previous occasion when she spoke well. She sounds triumphant at her success, not giving Leontes a chance to answer her questions. To some extent this short exchange between Hermione and Leontes echoes the tone of the longer dialogue between Hermione and Polixenes. She uses light-hearted, exaggerated terms but his images are more serious: 'Three crabbèd months'; and, much more bitter, 'had soured themselves to death'; and he finishes with a line which could be spoken as a warning, 'then didst thou utter, / "I am yours for ever." '

Hermione's words apparently give her husband and his friend equal status, but does she give a hand to each? Or does she give her hand first to her husband, then to Polixenes? Whichever a director decides, Hermione and Polixenes need to be holding hands in some way by line 115. Have they left Leontes by this point or does Leontes leave them? His passionate jealousy is immediate. Just what triggers it? It is important for the structure and the sense of the rest of the play that Hermione is not in any sense behaving licentiously, but there is a wide spectrum of possibilities open to the actors.

There is no development in Leontes' jealousy. He instantly assumes that Polixenes and Hermione have made love. Shakespeare's contemporaries believed that varieties of blood were mixed during sexual intercourse and Leontes' mind makes the leap between friendship and sex: 'To mingle friendship far is mingling bloods.' The rhythm of his speech is fragmented, reflecting the 'tremor cordis', the physical effects of his jealousy. He comments on their behaviour, the way they are holding hands ('paddling palms and pinching fingers') and looking at each other, in language which suggests sexuality and animal lust: 'and then to sigh, as 'twere / The mort [death] o'th'deer'.

The presence of Mamillius on stage is significant. Visually, the picture of Leontes removing a smudge from his child's face suggests paternal care. But Leontes is even questioning whether Mamillius is his son. Shakespeare's use of the child Mamillius is effective in showing how everything has become distorted in Leontes' perverse view of the world. Even language is no longer to be trusted. When he tells Mamillius that he must be clean, or 'neat', an alternative meaning comes into his mind. Shakespeare suggests that his jealousy has made him particularly sensitive to language so that the secondary meaning of 'neat' as horned cattle immediately suggests cuckold to Leontes' mind.

He acknowledges that Mamillius looks like him, in spite of the fact that 'Women say so, / That will say anything.' For Leontes, now that Hermione is false, all women are false. Mamillius' regenerative powers, referred to in Scene 1, almost begin to have an effect as he looks at his father with his heavenly blue ('welkin') eye, and Leontes starts to question the truth of his suspicions: 'Can thy dam? May't be?'

In one of the most discussed speeches of the play (lines 138–46) Leontes creates his own logic. He decides that since passion can influence dreams and the imagination (the 'unreal'), then passion can also affect the real, and he fully believes that it has. A key phrase here is 'infection of my brains', as it does seem that Leontes has a diseased imagination which takes him to the very edge of sanity. The broken syntax and incoherence of this speech are a vivid evocation of the confusion of his thoughts.

On stage, when do Polixenes and Hermione rejoin Leontes? His physical reaction to his suspicions is clearly evident to them: 'What means Sicilia?' asks Polixenes; 'Are you moved, my lord?' questions Hermione. As will continue to happen during this scene, Shakespeare colours Hermione's words with irony and shows Leontes taking them as an allusion to his all-too-clearly imagined cuckold's horns.

> You look
> As if you held a brow of much distraction. *(lines 148–9)*

Denying that he is disturbed in any way, Leontes makes a brief reference to his own 'tenderness' as 'folly' or foolishness, as though he feels that he has been mocked, or made 'a pastime / To harder bosoms'. Then, triggered by the presence of Mamillius, Leontes recollects his own childhood and Polixenes speaks of his love for his own son. The images Polixenes creates recall the references to the regenerative powers of Mamillius from Scene 1, lines 28–38, and the innocence of boyhood earlier in this scene. Shakespeare rarely uses young children on the stage, and the effect here of the closeness of father and son can be very moving in performance.

Leontes gives an ambiguous instruction to Hermione, 'How thou lov'st us show in our brother's welcome', and in an aside suggests to the audience that he is playing her like a fish on a line. Whatever the actors do as they leave the stage needs to reflect Leontes' description in some way, but the more chastely Hermione looks at Polixenes and holds his arm, the more it shows the extreme jealousy of Leontes.

Leontes' speech (lines 185–207), partly to his son, is full of graphic sexual imagery. It is packed with wordplay and alliteration which emphasises his disgust. Leontes puns bitterly on the various meanings of 'play': his son's playing, the sexual play of Hermione, and the part of cuckold that he has been forced to play which will destroy his reputation. Though he says 'there's comfort' in the fact that many other men have had the same experience, clearly he does not find it any consolation. There is a poignant moment when Mamillius replies to the last comprehensible thing his father says to him, in an effort to please him: 'I am like you, they say.'

When Camillo enters, Mamillius leaves, and in the exchange between the two men the audience can see just how far jealousy has corrupted Leontes' mind. He now thinks that everyone in the court knows what has been going on and that they are gossiping about him. Even language is corrupted for him as he assumes that Camillo's use of the word 'satisfy' can only imply sexual satisfaction. He cannot bring himself to speak openly of his suspicions and Camillo is forced to defend himself with dignity against a vague charge of disloyalty. In a speech (lines 267–78) that seems composed of fragments, there are two clear statements about Hermione, both vulgar euphemisms: 'My wife is slippery' and 'My wife's a hobby-horse'. Leontes then details what he has imagined Hermione and Polixenes doing and, with rising hysteria, reiterates 'nothing':

> Is this nothing?
> Why then the world and all that's in't is nothing,
> The covering sky is nothing, Bohemia nothing,
> My wife is nothing, nor nothing have these nothings,
> If this be nothing. *(lines 292–6)*

Even now Camillo has no idea about who is supposed to be Hermione's seducer. Leontes demands that Camillo should poison Polixenes, whom he now calls formally 'Bohemia'. Camillo makes every effort to change Leontes' mind but he is absolutely convinced that Hermione has been unfaithful. In Leontes' distorted view of the world, anyone who thinks differently is, by definition, a traitor. Camillo apparently agrees to poison Polixenes on condition that Leontes does nothing to cause any scandal concerning the queen and continues to appear friendly to Polixenes.

When Camillo is alone on stage he speaks of his dilemma in soliloquy. If he keeps his oath of allegiance he will commit murder. If he does not obey, Leontes will punish him. He decides his only recourse is to leave the court.

When Polixenes enters, his first words make it clear that Leontes was unable to behave normally; he describes Leontes' 'lip of much contempt'. Camillo is reluctant to say why Leontes has changed but eventually is forced to explain:

> He thinks, nay with all confidence he swears,
> As he had seen't, or been an instrument
> To vice you to't, that you have touched his queen
> Forbiddenly. *(lines 414–17)*

Polixenes is appalled by this imputation. If it were true he would be no better than Judas. Camillo urges they leave, and details his plan to ensure their safe escape. Polixenes immediately agrees to follow Camillo's suggestions and offers him a position of importance in his own court ('thy places shall / Still neighbour mine'). He is aware that if Leontes believes that Hermione has been unfaithful, his feelings of jealousy can only be increased if he thinks that his best friend has betrayed him. The language of the final lines creates a sense of haste:

POLIXENES   Let us avoid.
CAMILLO   It is in mine authority to command
            The keys of all the posterns. Please your highness
            To take the urgent hour. Come, sir, away!   *(lines 462–5)*

Act 1: Critical review

Act I sets up the potential tragedy of the play. Unlike *Othello*, which charts the growth of the love between Othello and Desdemona and explores the causes and effects of his jealousy, in *The Winter's Tale* the audience is given no warning of Leontes' sudden descent into jealousy. There is no gradual development of Leontes' jealousy; it just is.

Archidamus has been made to feel uncomfortable by the excessive hospitality of Sicilia, just as the oppressive courtesy shown to Polixenes embarrasses him. It is perhaps the excessive closeness between Polixenes and Leontes that adds to the emotional pressure in Act I. There are many images concerning their shared experiences as children together, and their continuing friendship, but a warning of the potentially flawed nature of their relationship is embodied in the language used to describe it.

The efforts made by Leontes, and especially Hermione, to change Polixenes' decision to leave go beyond what is reasonable, or good manners. He cannot, as a gentleman, refuse the pressure that Hermione puts on him: 'My prisoner, or my guest? By your dread "Verily", / One of them you shall be.' She claims that 'a lady's "Verily"'s / As potent as a lord's', but in this patriarchal society it is not. Her success in verbal persuasion, where her husband has failed, leads to her complete loss of power. Having striven so hard, and failed to persuade his friend to remain for an extra week, Leontes is taken aback by his wife's victory: 'At my request he would not.' His sudden descent into jealousy is spectacular and shocking. It seems close to madness. He cannot speak or think coherently. It is as though the whole security of his world has been lost if he cannot depend on the fidelity of Hermione. Without the ability to rely on the fixed points of his universe he feels betrayed by everyone. Even the regenerative powers of Mamillius cannot cure his 'diseased opinion'.

The extent of Leontes' emotional turmoil is shown by the way that he immediately considers murder as an option and orders Camillo, his closest adviser, to kill Polixenes. Camillo decides to leave the court in the company of Polixenes. The two men appear not to realise that they are abandoning Hermione to the full force of Leontes' rage.

Act 2 Scene 1

At the end of Act I the audience is aware that Polixenes has fled from Sicilia, therefore this quiet interlude is dramatically ironic since none of those on stage is aware of the enormity of what has happened. Shakespeare begins the scene in the middle of an exchange between Hermione, her ladies and Mamillius. Hermione is in the late stages of her pregnancy and is apparently finding the liveliness of her son an irritation. She asks her women to take care of him. Though the dialogue is in verse there is a sense of naturalism about the scene with the child. He is old enough to claim that he is no longer a baby but young enough to be gently teased by the ladies, who comment on Hermione's pregnancy: 'The queen your mother rounds apace.'

When Hermione is more comfortable she calls the child to her and asks him to tell her a story. She asks for a 'merry' tale but Mamillius says, 'A sad tale's best for winter.' This is a reminder of the play's title and the theme of seasonal regeneration, and also perhaps a warning to the audience of the sorrows to come. In order to prevent the ladies from hearing he sits close to his mother and whispers the story to her. Shakespeare, the actor's playwright, organises the stage image without recourse to stage directions. This allows the queen and the child to be plausibly engaged, not noticing the entrance of the king and his courtiers.

There is a sharp contrast between the quiet loving image of the mother and child and the abrupt invasion of this female space by Leontes and his lords. He fires an abrupt series of questions at his followers: 'Was he met there? His train? Camillo with him?' Through these three brief questions Shakespeare conveys the narrative to the audience.

Leontes describes his state of mind by comparing it to the revulsion felt by someone finding a spider in their drink, and to the myth that spiders were poisonous only if they were seen. He claims that if he had known nothing of Hermione's adultery he would have been still happy, but he has been sickened because he has 'drunk, and seen the spider'. His suspicions have spread and now he feels that there has been a 'plot against my life, my crown'. The anonymous lord, explaining why the city gates were unlocked, emphasises the high position Camillo has had to forfeit by leaving:

> By his great authority,
> Which often hath no less prevailed than so
> On your command. *(lines 53–5)*

Leontes takes the child from Hermione, referring again to his own image in the child. At this point Hermione thinks that Leontes is playing some kind of game: 'What is this? Sport?' Leontes turns her own word against her: 'let her sport herself / With that she's big with'. Leontes makes the accusation that his wife is pregnant by Polixenes as public as possible, using the assembled lords as his on-stage audience, inviting them to look at her, to comment on her beauty. His speech begins formally, 'Look on her, mark her well', but as he comes closer to his final accusation, and has to express what he believes her to be, he loses fluency. For the first time he uses an explicit statement rather than a euphemism: 'She's an adultress'.

Hermione's refutation is made directly to Leontes: 'You, my lord, / Do but mistake.' His reply throws her word back to her: 'You have mistook, my lady, / Polixenes for Leontes.' He goes on to abuse her, calling her 'thing', rather than 'lady' because she has abused 'degrees' or hierarchy. He reiterates the accusation that she has committed adultery and that she is a traitor. Camillo is also accused of both treachery and knowledge of her infidelity. Again Hermione speaks directly to Leontes in her denial, unselfishly thinking of his grief when he realises his 'mistake'. Ironically her words will come all too true when Leontes finally realises the devastation his jealousy has brought upon him. But that lies in the future, and now in a speech which recalls Act 1 Scene 2, lines 292–6, Leontes speaks of his absolute conviction:

> No; if I mistake
> In those foundations which I build upon,
> The centre is not big enough to bear
> A schoolboy's top. *(lines 100–3)*

Hearing that she must be imprisoned, Hermione with dignity then addresses the lords, and accepts the decision of the king. She assumes control of her own arrest, 'The king's will be performed!', so that Leontes is left demanding 'Shall I be heard?' She maintains authority, choosing her own time to leave, accompanied by her women. It is only when Hermione has left the stage that any of the lords speak in her defence. Antigonus is the most blunt. He insists on Hermione's innocence, threatening first to chain his wife to him to ensure that she cannot betray him. In an even more outrageous image, he says that if Hermione proves to be false he will castrate all three of his daughters – or even himself; 'I had rather glib myself than they / Should not produce fair issue'.

Antigonus and Leontes have an increasingly acerbic argument until Leontes changes the tone by using the royal 'we' and speaking more formally and rhetorically. Antigonus refuses to be intimidated. Leontes announces that he has sent Cleomenes and Dion to Apollo's shrine at Delphos for 'spiritual counsel'. It is clear from his final speech in the scene that he expects confirmation of Hermione's guilt and that he conceives the function of the oracle to be to maintain public order by its endorsement of his decision. The scene ends on a lighter note from Antigonus, who clearly expects the oracle to vindicate Hermione and make Leontes a laughing-stock:

> To laughter, as I take it,
> If the good truth were known.   *(lines 198–9)*

Act 2 Scene 2

Shakespeare lets the audience know from the first line where the scene is to be set: 'The keeper of the prison, call to him.' Paulina is the wife of Antigonus, and she is even more forthright than her husband. She browbeats the gaoler into allowing her to see Emilia, one of the queen's ladies. Emilia tells her that Hermione has had a daughter: 'a goodly babe, / Lusty, and like to live'. Paulina says that she will inform the king that he has a child and intends to make it clear to him that he has made a mistake in imprisoning his wife: 'If I prove honey-mouthed, let my tongue blister'. She believes that the king will 'soften at the sight o'th'child'. Emilia tells her that Hermione had already thought of sending the baby to see the king but was not sure whom to choose as a messenger. The gaoler is not sure that he should allow the baby to leave the prison but Paulina overrides his protests. Her justification appeals to the power of nature, which is part of the wider theme of the cycle of seasonal regeneration:

This child was prisoner to the womb, and is
By law and process of great nature thence
Freed and enfranchised   *(lines 59–61)*

Act 2 Scene 3

Leontes begins the scene with a shocking soliloquy that expresses his
tortured mind. He imagines that wreaking dreadful vengeance on
Hermione will help him. He cannot sleep, something he has already
referred to in Act 1 Scene 2 when he spoke of the 'sullying' of
the 'purity and whiteness' of his sheets (lines 325–9). Now he has no
peace: 'Nor night nor day no rest.' He decides that, though Polixenes
'the harlot king' is beyond his reach, he can be revenged on
Hermione:

                    say that she were gone,
        Given to the fire, a moiety of my rest
        Might come to me again.   *(lines 7–9)*

When the servant enters with news of Mamillius' illness, Leontes
ascribes it to Hermione's loss of honour. He is disturbed by this, and
by the thought that Camillo and Polixenes must be laughing at him:
'make their pastime at my sorrow'. This makes him even more
determined to take revenge on Hermione. He intends to ensure that
she will experience the full weight of his vengeance.

The assembled lords attending on Leontes seem unable to prevent
the entrance of Paulina with the baby. She tells them it is their fault
that Leontes is unable to sleep and that their excessive obedience
fosters 'the cause of his awaking'. Her intention is to speak the truth
plainly to Leontes, 'to purge him of that humour / That presses him
from sleep'. She seems perhaps too forthright when she announces to
Leontes that she has come to discuss 'gossips' (godparents) for the
child. Though the verbal duel is between Leontes and Paulina, he does
not speak to her, but to Antigonus whom he blames for her presence.
She replies directly to his accusations; in contrast he speaks to
Antigonus, accusing him of failing to control his wife: 'Thou dotard,
thou art woman-tired, unroosted / By thy Dame Partlet here.' He
orders Antigonus to 'Take up the bastard', but Paulina places her
husband in a difficult position by telling him:

For ever

Unvenerable be thy hands if thou
Tak'st up the princess by that forcèd baseness
Which he has put upon't!   *(lines 76–9)*

Paulina accuses Leontes of being the only traitor present because his allegations have betrayed the honour of his queen and his children. He continues to avoid addressing her, and instructs the lords: 'Hence with it, and together with the dam / Commit them to the fire!' She ignores his threats and insists that the child is his own, pointing out its likeness to him as evidence of its parentage. This insistence that the child is a copy of its father echoes the way that Leontes found it comforting that Mamillius was said to be like him, which he mentioned several times in Act 1 Scene 2. Paulina calls upon 'good goddess Nature' who has made the baby look like Leontes, to ensure that the child's mind is free from similar suspicions (though Paulina expresses it in a strange fashion: 'lest she suspect, as he does, / Her children not her husband's'). Again Leontes instructs Antigonus to remove his wife, then for the first time he speaks to her directly: 'I'll ha' thee burnt.' Paulina shows great courage in her immediate response: 'I care not'. Yet again Leontes seems unable to enforce his threat, turning again to Antigonus and demanding, 'On your allegiance, / Out of the chamber with her!' Shakespeare includes stage directions in Paulina's response as she withdraws leaving the baby on stage:

I pray you do not push me, I'll be gone.
Look to your babe, my lord; 'tis yours. Jove send her
A better guiding spirit! What needs these hands?   *(lines 124–6)*

Leontes turns on Antigonus with renewed anger, ordering him to see that the child is burnt. If he refuses, not only will Leontes execute him and confiscate all his property, but he will dash out the brains of the child himself. On their knees, the lords beg Leontes to relent, and briefly he does so: 'But be it; let it live.' However he immediately changes his mind and asks Antigonus what he would venture to save the child's life. Antigonus takes a risk, swearing to do anything before he knows what he is committing himself to. Leontes' language changes to the formal speech appropriate to the oath that has been taken by Antigonus. Using the royal 'we', he instructs Antigonus to take the child and abandon it in a foreign country, 'Where chance may nurse or end it'. Antigonus has no choice, and he takes the child, recalling as he does so the legends of animals caring for abandoned children.

After Antigonus has left the stage the tone abruptly changes. A servant announces the imminent return of Cleomenes and Dion from Delphos. Leontes is pleased, thinking that this will resolve everything for him. He expects confirmation of Hermione's guilt but promises she shall have a fair trial, even though he clearly expects it is only by her death that his tortured mind will be eased:

> for as she hath
> Been publicly accused, so shall she have
> A just and open trial. While she lives
> My heart will be a burden to me.   *(lines 202–5)*

Act 2: Critical review

Dramatically, the audience's knowledge of Leontes' fury casts an ominous shadow over this opening episode. The tranquil atmosphere in the women's apartments as Mamillius tells his story privately to his mother changes abruptly; Leontes enters this feminine environment with his lords and Hermione is exposed to the harsh irrational violence of Leontes' temper. Hermione does not lose dignity in spite of all the public insults thrown at her by Leontes and almost takes charge of the situation by facing him with dignity. She is watched by her women and by the silent chorus of Leontes' lords, who do not speak in her defence until she is gone. When Leontes cannot win the argument because he has no proof of Hermione's guilt, he resorts to force, ordering Hermione's imprisonment.

The short episode in the prison vividly establishes Paulina's character and reputation. She bullies the gaoler into allowing her to take the baby to Leontes, though he has no warrant to do so. Paulina's words about the child being 'Freed and enfranchised' by nature remind the audience that there are powers greater than the temporal authority of the king.

In Scene 3 there can be an underlying thread of humour in performance, as all the men, even Leontes, seem afraid of Paulina. Her husband, the lords and the servant all try ineffectually to keep her from Leontes' presence. Her character has affinities with Noah's wife from the Mystery Plays, who wields power with her tongue; but in other ways she is one of the strongest and most steadfast of the women in Shakespeare's plays. Paulina speaks for common sense. In contrast, the men seem to be very aware of the hierarchical structure of the court and of the consequent obligations to be obedient to the desires of the king, however bizarre the state of the king's mind.

Throughout the conversation with Paulina, Antigonus and the lords, Leontes refuses to acknowledge the baby's humanity. He calls the child, 'bastard . . . it . . . brat'. His final judgement that the child must be cast out in 'some remote and desert place' seems worse than 'a present death', but there is a suggestion that all may yet be well when the return of Cleomenes and Dion from Delphi is announced.

Act 3 Scene 1

In this short scene, Cleomenes and Dion, Leontes' messengers, are discussing their impressions of their visit to Apollo's shrine. Cleomenes describes the beauty of the island and its fertility. His words carry great significance because they express one of the major themes of the play, the beneficence of nature. Dion speaks about the 'celestial habits' of the attendants of the shrine and 'the reverence / Of the grave wearers'. The language they use stresses the calm and peaceful atmosphere of the island, and the holiness of the shrine. Shakespeare enhances the tone of tranquillity by the way that each man completes the other's lines. They speak of their experience as being 'rare' and 'pleasant', and they pray that it will prove beneficial to the queen: 'Great Apollo / Turn all to th'best!'

Shakespeare also uses the scene to convey information. Their conversation suggests that there are notices ('proclamations') all over Sicilia accusing Hermione of treachery, and their confidence that the message will 'clear or end the business' seems designed to reinforce the audience's trust in the oracle, 'Thus by Apollo's great divine sealed up'. There is an increased sense of prophecy in the idea expressed by Dion, 'Something rare / Even then will rush to knowledge.' Though the tone of this scene has been predominantly reflective and tranquil, Dion's final lines emphasise the haste of their journey back to Leontes:

> Go; fresh horses,
> And gracious be the issue!   *(lines 21–2)*

Act 3 Scene 2

This trial scene is one of the great set-piece scenes of the play however simply it is staged. Leontes begins the proceedings with a formal opening speech. He makes it clear that he feels he is holding an open trial to avoid any claims that he is tyrannical, and that he will 'Proceed in justice'. Although in Acts 1 and 2 he has made the audience aware of his conviction that Hermione is guilty, now he claims publicly that the trial will lead to 'the guilt or the purgation' of Hermione.

The officer reads Hermione's indictment. It accuses her of adultery, of conspiracy with Polixenes and Camillo to murder Leontes and of assisting them to escape. Hermione's first speech in her own defence is measured and dignified. She is aware that she has no evidence to offer, and that Leontes will interpret whatever she says as a lie:

> Mine integrity,
> Being counted falsehood, shall, as I express it,
> Be so received. *(lines 24–6)*

She has no doubt that 'powers divine' are witnesses to her innocence. Her appeal to Leontes is grounded on his knowledge of her character, though she knows that he will refuse to acknowledge it. She describes her situation as being more unhappy 'Than history can pattern, though devised / And played to take spectators'. Her words claim that her misery has no historical parallel. They also ironically refer to the fact that the onlookers on stage, and the audience in the auditorium, are indeed witnessing her unhappiness.

Hermione proudly declares that she is both a queen and a daughter of a king, but she says that she is defending herself principally for the sake of the honour of her children. She appeals to Leontes' conscience to state precisely how she has transgressed. She is prepared to risk the condemnation of everyone, even of her own family, if she has stepped beyond the bounds of honour in either thought or deed. Leontes is abruptly dismissive of her defence.

Hermione deals with the accusations against her point by point. She admits that she loved Polixenes, but only 'in honour'. She reminds Leontes that earlier (Act 1 Scene 2, lines 173–4) he had instructed her to love Polixenes:

> I do confess
> I loved him as in honour he required:
> With such a kind of love as might become
> A lady like me, with a love even such,
> So and no other, as yourself commanded *(lines 60–4)*

She also refutes the charge of conspiracy saying that Camillo 'was an honest man'. Leontes refuses to believe her. His refusal and his repeated accusations prompt Hermione to protest: 'You speak a language that I understand not'. This identification of the way Leontes twists the meaning of words as a direct result of his imagined cuckoldry is strikingly perceptive, particularly as it is immediately followed by an example of such obsessional wordplay. Hermione says, 'My life stands in the level of your dreams, / Which I'll lay down.' To which Leontes passionately exclaims:

> Your actions are my dreams.   *(line 80)*

Leontes interprets her words to mean that she is saying her actions exist only in his imagination, which is of course true, though he cannot believe it.

Leontes' passionate response that her 'actions are my dreams', shows how Shakespeare deepens thematic resonance. For Leontes, the infidelity of Hermione is so devastating that nothing, not even language, is reliable. The reference to dreams also recalls the opening of Act 2 Scene 3 ('Nor night nor day no rest'). Leontes grows increasingly angry as he tells her that her baby has been 'cast out' and that she will be executed. Hermione's reply is dignified and courageous.

> Sir, spare your threats.
> The bug which you would fright me with, I seek.   *(lines 89–90)*

She lists all the things that she has lost through Leontes' jealousy: his love, the presence of her son, her baby, her reputation, her health after the birth of her child, then asks him:

> Now, my liege,
> Tell me what blessings I have here alive
> That I should fear to die.   *(lines 104–6)*

Knowing that Leontes will not change his mind, she asks for judgement from the oracle: 'Apollo be my judge!'

It is one of the unnamed lords, not Leontes, who acknowledges the justice of her request and orders the sealed message from the oracle to be brought into the court. Just as in Scene 1, Shakespeare emphasises the holiness of the oracle by the ritual surrounding it. Cleomenes and Dion swear that the seals are unbroken. Various directors have ensured that the special nature of the message is conveyed to the audience as strikingly as possible. One production had it sealed in a pottery vessel which was smashed on the floor to reveal the message from the oracle. Traditionally, messages from Apollo's oracle were vague, capable of a variety of interpretations, but this message is remarkably clear. Only the final phrase seems equivocal: 'if that which is lost be not found'. Hermione and the lords are overjoyed but Leontes refuses to believe even the words of Apollo. Shakespeare seems to be emphasising Leontes' extreme paranoia. He is obsessed by his jealousy:

> There is no truth at all i'th'oracle!
> The sessions shall proceed: this is mere falsehood. *(lines 137–8)*

Immediately Leontes has committed the sacrilege of disbelief in the oracle a messenger arrives with the news of the death of his son. Leontes instantly realises the consequences of his madness: 'the heavens themselves / Do strike at my injustice'. Hermione faints and is carried off stage. As quickly as it had arrived, Leontes' jealousy disappears: 'I have too much believed mine own suspicion.' The actor playing Leontes is faced with the difficult task of making his sudden remorse credible as he lists the actions he will undertake to put things right:

> I'll reconcile me to Polixenes,
> New woo my queen, recall the good Camillo,
> Whom I proclaim a man of truth, of mercy *(lines 152–4)*

Leontes is still explaining how good Camillo was when Paulina rushes back on stage lamenting. Though a lord asks, 'What fit is this, good lady?', she does not reply but demands of Leontes: 'What studied torments, tyrant, hast for me?' She calls him a 'fool', 'inconstant, / And damnable ingrateful', less compassionate than a devil, 'a gross and foolish sire', and angrily lists the effects of his jealousy. She declares that none of the things he has done is important compared to the fact that the queen is dead. Shakespeare withholds the most important lines of Paulina's speech to the very end to give maximum impact to the information.

Those on stage are shocked and cannot believe her words, but Paulina reiterates that the queen is dead and calls on Leontes to despair, and the audience is reminded that this is a sad tale, best for winter.

> A thousand knees,
> Ten thousand years together, naked, fasting,
> Upon a barren mountain, and still winter
> In storm perpetual, could not move the gods
> To look that way thou wert.   *(lines 207–11)*

Leontes does not say how he will right the wrongs he has done. Rather he asks her to continue to rebuke him. There are no stage directions for Leontes' behaviour but the actor must show a depth of remorse that evokes even Paulina's pity. Shakespeare gives the actor few words here:

> Go on, go on.
> Thou canst not speak too much; I have deserved
> All tongues to talk their bitt'rest.   *(lines 211–13)*

Paulina comments that, 'He is touched / To th'noble heart', and even as she tries to comfort him realises that any mention of the results of his jealous actions brings more pain to Leontes and she promises to 'say nothing'.

The scene ends with Leontes vowing to weep daily at the chapel where his wife and son are buried.

> Come, and lead me
> To these sorrows.   *(lines 239–40)*

Act 3 Scene 3

The scene abruptly shifts to Bohemia. Because there would be no scenery to suggest the location on the stage in Shakespeare's time, Bohemia is mentioned in Antigonus' first speech. The storm imagined by Paulina in the previous scene seems to be threatening here, and as the scene develops the storm increases. The Mariner sets the scene for the audience as he describes the weather in detail and tells of the reputation the coast has for 'creatures / Of prey'. The Mariner feels that the stormy weather is an indication that the gods are angry with them for abandoning the baby.

Antigonus' long narrative soliloquy describes his vivid dream. Hermione has appeared to him, 'In pure white robes, / Like very sanctity', and instructed him to leave the child in Bohemia and to call it Perdita (the lost one). She told him that he will never see his wife again. Though Antigonus claims not to trust in dreams, he is obeying the instructions 'superstitiously'. Antigonus questions his experience, and decides that it was not just a dream and that Hermione's ghost really did appear to him: 'This was so, and no slumber'. He believes that the apparition is evidence that Hermione is dead, and that Apollo wishes that the child should be abandoned 'upon the earth / Of its right father'. He leaves a box and papers with the child. He feels that Leontes' commands have made him 'accursed'.

The storm increases, and Antigonus also hears the noise of an approaching hunt: 'This is the chase!' He sees the approach of a bear and flees the stage in the knowledge that he will die: 'I am gone for ever!'

Exit, pursued by a bear   (line 57)

This is one of the most famous stage directions written by Shakespeare and one of the most challenging for a director. Almost anything that a modern director decides to do with this stage direction is likely to generate laughter from the audience, rather than the fear and pity almost certainly intended by Shakespeare. Some directors have anticipated the probable laughter and deliberately prompted it by having an actor costumed as a pantomime bear; others have avoided the problem by using lighting and sound effects. One production had Leontes appear on stage, Antigonus kneel to kiss his hand and then Leontes kill Antigonus with a swipe of his hand in a bear's paw glove.

As the storm subsides, the mood of the play also changes with the entrance of a Shepherd, looking for his sheep. He speaks the perennial criticism of the young by the old; young men should 'sleep' between the ages of 10 and 23, 'for there is nothing in the between but getting wenches with child, wronging the ancientry, stealing, fighting'. His humour and down-to-earth common sense provide relief after the tension of the court scenes and Antigonus' terror. He finds the baby and from the quality of its clothing assumes that it is the illegitimate child of a waiting-gentlewoman. He decides to 'take it up for pity', and calls for his son.

There is a marked contrast between the dreadful fate of Antigonus as witnessed by the audience and the way that the Shepherd's son describes it. The son, often designated 'Clown' in the stage directions, or sometimes 'Young Shepherd', is a simple peasant. He humorously describes the storm and the sinking of the ship with all hands, and the way that Antigonus is torn apart by the bear. He tells how little time has passed since he saw both events: 'The men are not yet cold under water, nor the bear half dined on the gentleman'.

The Shepherd seems to take the news no more seriously than his son:

> Thou met'st with things dying, I with things new born.
>
> *(lines 100–1)*

This is often taken to be the turning point of the play, marking the symbolic shift from the tragic events that took place in Sicilia to the regeneration which will occur in Bohemia. The Shepherd shows his son the child, which they both assume to be a changeling. The box is full of gold and they think it is a gift to them from the fairies. In spite of their good fortune they remember the fate of Antigonus, and the Clown says before he goes home he will see if there is enough left of him to bury.

Act 3: Critical review

The final lines of Act 2 reported news of Cleomenes and Dion's return, but the beginning of Act 3 has them still on their way to Leontes' court. Their description of Delphi suggests that they have been successful. Their emphasis on the sanctity of the temple, and the impression of piety that they convey, implies that the oracle will have good news.

The trial is public and conducted in formal language. Hermione is articulate in her defence but knows that she can bring no proof of her innocence, only her denial which Leontes will not believe. As the trial progresses, the dramatic focus closes in. Leontes becomes less like a judge and rails at Hermione with passionate anger. The audience, on stage and off, shares Hermione's relief at the unambiguous message from the oracle. Shockingly, Leontes denies its truth and the speed of the action accelerates as a servant announces the death of Mamillius. Hermione faints and is carried off stage. When Paulina returns with news of Hermione's death, Leontes can say nothing except to encourage her to lay all blame on him. There is an ironic echo of Mamillius' 'A sad tale's best for winter' when Paulina implies that Leontes' actions have brought winter to Sicilia.

The audience's belief that Hermione is dead is confirmed by Antigonus' dream. Antigonus obeys the instructions given by the spirit of Hermione. Believing that Polixenes has fathered the child, Antigonus leaves it on the coast of Bohemia in a tempestuous storm. His terrible death is preceded by the stage direction: '*Exit, pursued by a bear*'.

Now that the action has moved to Bohemia, the atmosphere changes. The Shepherd and the Clown, neither given a name, bring a more earthy kind of humour to the play. The Clown's jumbled accounts of the shocking deaths that he has witnessed serve to distance the audience from some of the horror. The Shepherd draws attention to the end of the tragedy and the beginning of the comic element of the play with its promise of future hope:

Thou met'st with things dying, I with things new born.

Act 4 Scene 1

Shakespeare gives no indications about the appearance of Time, and directors have found various inventive ways of presenting the speech. One company shared out the lines between the actors who were completing their costume changes to appear in Bohemia; another had Time spoken as a rap; another had Camillo bursting a balloon in which he found the speech, and another shared the appropriate lines between Mamillius, Perdita, the Shepherd and Polixenes.

It is spoken in 16 rhyming couplets to represent the 16 years that have passed. Very few lines are end-stopped and the smooth rhythm invites the actor to deliver it as a conversation with the audience. In the first 15 lines, Time speaks of his powers and asks the audience's indulgence to imagine the passing of 16 years. He tells that he has been the unchanging witness of the past and of the present. In the centre of the speech, Time uses the traditional hourglass image of the passing of time: 'I turn my glass'. Now his tale is of the present. He speaks of leaving Leontes secluded in his grief and asks the audience to imagine that Time is now in Bohemia. For the first time the audience learns the name of Polixenes' son: Florizel. Time says that the rest of his story concerns Perdita, who is living as a shepherd's daughter in Bohemia. He says that she is 'now grown in grace', an image that echoes the references to grace associated with Hermione. Time finishes his speech with a conventional disclaimer, asking for the indulgence of the audience, and so acknowledging the fictional and theatrical qualities of what they are watching.

Act 4 Scene 2

Camillo was one of the courtiers who opened *The Winter's Tale* and spoke of the close relationship between the kings. Here, he seems to open the second half of the play in a similar way. In Act 1 Camillo was spoken of as Leontes' closest adviser and, having engineered Polixenes' escape, he now appears to be fulfilling that role for him. Camillo is eager to return to Sicilia. He says that 'the penitent king, my master' has sent for him and he wishes to be of comfort to Leontes. Polixenes is now placed in the position of persuading someone to stay against his will and he does not want Camillo to leave: 'Better not to have had thee than thus to want thee.' He says that Camillo's services are essential. Polixenes begs Camillo not to mention Sicilia, 'that fatal country', as it fills him with fresh grief.

Polixenes asks Camillo if he has seen Florizel, whom he blames for 'not being gracious'. Both men have noticed that Florizel has been absent from the court and 'less frequent to his princely exercises than formerly'. Polixenes has spies ('eyes under my service') who have told him that Florizel often visits a 'most homely shepherd' who has grown unaccountably wealthy. Camillo has also heard this rumour and has also heard of the beauty of the shepherd's daughter. Polixenes fears that she plans to entrap Florizel ('the angle that plucks our son thither') and asks Camillo to go with him, in disguise, to see the Shepherd and learn the truth about Florizel.

Act 4 Scene 3

This scene opens with a song, the first in the play, and it establishes the lighter tone of the country scene in Bohemia. Autolycus sings of the seasons, beginning with spring, 'the sweet o'the year', marking the end of the sad tale of the 'winter's pale'. He also sings of his trade, which is stealing. At some time in the past he has been in the service of Prince Florizel and has worn expensive 'three-pile' velvet, but now he is a petty thief: 'a snapper-up of unconsidered trifles', a gambler, and a con-man: 'my revenue is the silly cheat'. He is afraid of punishment but not of hell. When the Shepherd's son, the Clown, comes along on his way to market he is immediately proclaimed as a 'prize' by Autolycus.

The Clown is trying to work out the profit that his father has made on the sheep-shearing, but his arithmetic is not up to it. Autolycus listens to his talk of profit and plans to trap him like a foolish woodcock. The Clown goes through his shopping list, which includes items unusually exotic and expensive for a simple sheep-farmer's feast to celebrate the success of the shearing. His description makes it clear that the feast is to be elaborate because his father has made his sister 'mistress of the feast' and she spares no expense.

Autolycus' pretence of being the victim of a robbery gives the actors the opportunity for visual action to enhance the comedy. The Clown takes every exaggeration that Autolycus makes with great seriousness and sympathy: 'Alas, poor man, a million of beating may come to a great matter.' Autolycus shows how accurate his self-assessment was when he described himself as a 'snapper-up of unconsidered trifles', or an opportunist thief. He has overheard the Clown planning his spending, so he picks his pocket, saying ironically, 'You ha' done me a charitable office.' The Clown may be simple but he is indeed charitable, and Autolycus has trouble avoiding the Clown's discovering his loss when he tries to give money to Autolycus. Again this gives scope for stage business as Autolycus tries to stop the Clown searching his pockets for money. Autolycus describes the man who attacked him, and in doing so describes himself, confident that the Clown will not know him. The audience becomes aware that Autolycus is talking about himself as someone who has been dismissed from the court for his 'virtues'. The Clown corrects him, 'His vices, you would say', and makes an unintentionally ironic reference to the inability of the courtiers to keep virtue in the court. This is more likely to be Shakespeare's joke about the contemporary court of King James I than a reference to the court of Polixenes.

Autolycus lists the various ways he has tried to make money, none of them settled jobs. He says that he has now 'settled only in rogue'. His reputation must have spread far and wide because even the Clown has heard of him and knows where he is to be found. Autolycus admits to being a coward when the Clown tells him that he should have 'looked big and spit at him'. The dramatic irony of this scene depends on Autolycus' effrontery and the actor's ability to engage the audience's complicity in his deceit. Though the Clown is a figure of fun because he is simple and easily duped, he is also good-hearted and even offers to escort Autolycus further on his journey. When he refuses, the Clown goes off to market, leaving Autolycus alone on stage to revel in his theft and the fact that he has another deception planned at the sheep-shearing festivities:

> If I make not this cheat bring out another, and the shearers
> prove sheep, let me be unrolled and my name put in the book
> of virtue.   (lines 105–6)

Act 4 Scene 4

The first exchange between Florizel and Perdita is striking. They speak in courtly verse, and each is dressed unusually; Florizel is dressed as a shepherd, 'obscured / With a swain's wearing', and Perdita as the queen of the sheep-shearing feast, 'Most goddess-like pranked up'. Shakespeare's original audience would have recognised in them the conventional figures from the pastoral ideal (see page 61). Florizel praises Perdita, comparing her to Flora, the goddess of the

Spring. Perdita emphasises their difference in status by calling Florizel 'The gracious mark o'th'land' and herself 'poor lowly maid'. They speak of their first meeting, apparently by chance when Florizel was hawking, and Perdita expresses her fear that chance may reveal their meetings to the king. She is concerned about Polixenes' reaction to finding his son in the arms of a shepherdess:

> How would he look to see his work, so noble,
> Vilely bound up? *(lines 21–2)*

Florizel comforts her. He justifies their love using classical references, referring to Jupiter, Neptune and Apollo, who all disguised themselves for love. The references might seem ironic because the 'transformations' of these gods were for purposes of seduction rather than marriage. But Florizel assures Perdita that not only is she more beautiful than the mortals desired by the gods but that his love is honourable. She seems much more realistic when she reminds him that the king would not permit him to marry her:

> Your resolution cannot hold when 'tis
> Opposed, as it must be, by th'power of the king. *(lines 36–7)*

Florizel tries to persuade Perdita to forget her fears and to celebrate the feast. He makes a commitment to be faithful to her:

> Or I'll be thine, my fair,
> Or not my father's; for I cannot be
> Mine own, nor anything to any, if
> I be not thine. *(lines 42–5)*

When the guests for the feast arrive he urges her to be as happy as if it were their wedding day.

The tone changes from intimate and tender to festive public celebration when the Shepherd and the other country guests arrive, with Polixenes and Camillo in disguise. By dramatic convention even the smallest disguise is assumed to be totally impenetrable on stage, and Florizel does not recognise his father and Camillo. The Shepherd describes the cheerfully vulgar way his 'old wife' behaved at such feasts and briskly tells Perdita to behave as the 'Mistress o'th'Feast'. Her response to this is dignified and sophisticated. She welcomes

Polixenes and Camillo with gifts of rosemary and rue, herbs that traditionally symbolise remembering and grace (though rue can also suggest bitter repentance). As these herbs retain their scent when stored, Polixenes assumes that she has given them 'flowers of winter' in reference to their age. Perdita's reply is the beginning of what is often referred to as the debate between the merits of nature and nurture, which is one of the key themes of the play (see page 60).

Perdita begins the argument by excusing her gift of herbs on the grounds that the prettiest flowers in season are

> carnations and streaked gillyvors,
> Which some call nature's bastards   *(lines 82–3)*

She says that she will not grow them because their cultivation depends on human interference with 'great creating nature'. This image echoes Paulina's reasoning at Perdita's birth (Act 2 Scene 2, line 60). In a modern dress production, as she spoke Perdita handed Polixenes a leaflet criticising genetically modified foods. It was a piece of stage business intended to demonstrate the continuing relevance of the debate. Polixenes defends human intervention by arguing that the only way nature can be improved is by using natural devices:

> Yet nature is made better by no mean
> But nature makes that mean; so over that art,
> Which you say adds to nature, is an art
> That nature makes.   *(lines 89–92)*

Polixenes uses the image of marriage to give the sense of an improved offspring from grafting 'a bark of baser kind' on to a 'bud of nobler race'. Shakespeare makes clear the explicit connection between the discussion about gardening and the reason for the presence of Polixenes at the sheep-shearing feast; he fears that his noble son has been entrapped by a base shepherdess. Polixenes and Perdita each appear to be arguing against their own interests.

Perdita seems to agree with Polixenes, but when he advises her to plant gillyvors she makes a forthright speech of refusal:

> I'll not put
> The dibble in earth to set one slip of them   *(lines 99–100)*

Her comparison with cosmetics makes it clear that she thinks of Polixenes' word 'art' as artifice. Her language is just as unambiguously direct:

> No more than, were I painted, I would wish
> This youth should say 'twere well, and only therefore
> Desire to breed by me. *(lines 101–3)*

Though the words she uses are down-to-earth, Perdita's behaviour and ability to argue her point of view suggest that Shakespeare intends the audience to remember that she is the daughter of a king. She shows courtesy to the unknown guests at the feast and offers them 'flowers / Of middle summer' to close the discussion. Camillo seems smitten by Perdita's beauty and attempts a weak complimentary pun:

> I should leave grazing, were I of your flock,
> And only live by gazing. *(lines 109–10)*

Perdita speaks of her wish for appropriate flowers to give to Florizel and the shepherdesses to suit their youth. She makes references to the classical myth of Proserpina in her descriptions of the flowers. It is dangerous to give naturalistic biographies to characters in Shakespeare's plays (see pages 87–8, 119) but he again seems to be suggesting that Perdita's sophisticated knowledge and manners are innate. Perdita claims that she feels she is acting ('I play as I have seen them do / In Whitsun pastorals') and that it is her unaccustomed dress which changes her 'disposition'.

In an elaborate response, using simple words but powerful repetitions and imagery, Florizel praises Perdita's speaking, singing and dancing. He claims that everything she does is exemplary:

> Each your doing,
> So singular in each particular,
> Crowns what you are doing in the present deeds,
> That all your acts are queens. *(lines 143–6)*

For the first time, the audience learns Florizel's assumed name, Doricles. Perdita feels that he is praising her too extravagantly and that she would be afraid he was wooing her with flattery if he were not so transparently honourable. In a vivid image of turtledoves who were believed to mate for life, Florizel makes another reference to their commitment to each other: 'so turtles pair / That never mean to part'.

Dramatically, the focus on stage moves briefly to Polixenes and Camillo, who comment on Perdita. Polixenes praises Perdita as 'the prettiest low-born lass' and, like his son, observes that:

> Nothing she does or seems
> But smacks of something greater than herself,
> Too noble for this place.   (lines 157–9)

Camillo's observation of Florizel and Perdita gives them implicit stage directions and interprets their actions for the audience: 'He tells her something / That makes her blood look out.'

After the intimacy of the exchanges between Perdita and the three men, again the focus and the tone change abruptly to physical celebration as the Clown demands music. Mopsa and Dorcas argue, and remind the audience of the difference between the language and manners of Perdita and these two shepherdesses who display the conventional stage behaviour of peasant characters. The dance here is both a rustic entertainment and an echo of the dances which were part of courtly entertainment. The dance has been presented on stage in many different ways, ranging from a very brief interlude to a lengthy choreographed set piece.

Polixenes takes the opportunity to question the Shepherd about 'Doricles'. The Shepherd seems pleased with his daughter's choice and he comments on Doricles' honest appearance: 'He looks like sooth'. The Shepherd also comments on the love that Perdita and Doricles have for each other:

> to be plain,
> I think there is not half a kiss to choose
> Who loves another best.   (lines 174–6)

Polixenes' brief response ('She dances featly') can be said in a number of ways and perhaps gives the actor an opportunity to remind the audience of his true identity. A different possible reminder of past events occurs in the Shepherd's words:

> she shall bring him that
> Which he not dreams of. *(lines 179–80)*

Shakespeare delays any further discussion of the relationship between Florizel and Perdita by reintroducing Autolycus. An excited servant rushes onto the stage with an enthusiastic description of the pedlar at the door. The tone is also changed by the shift to prose. The servant speaks of the pedlar's skill in singing; 'as he had eaten ballads'. He comments on the variety of his love-songs, though his detailed insistence on their lack of 'bawdry' or obscenity makes it clear that the songs are full of indecent references. Polixenes comments ironically on the foolishness of the servant; 'This is a brave fellow', but the Clown is thoroughly impressed and asks for more detail. The servant has been won over by the pedlar's sales talk and says that he has an indescribable quantity of things for sale. When the Clown asks the servant to bring in the pedlar it is significant that Perdita has had a more perceptive understanding of the servant's description. She asks the servant to 'Forewarn him that he use no scurrilous words in's tunes.'

When Autolycus comes on stage, wearing a disguise, the audience becomes aware that he has invested the money stolen from the Clown in a full pedlar's pack. He enters singing a song praising the quality of his goods, making them all sound luxuriously desirable. The Clown is instantly taken in, and because he is in love with Mopsa intends to buy ribbons and gloves for her. This sparks off a squabble between Mopsa and Dorcas full of sexual innuendo. Dorcas implies that the Clown has promised to sleep with Mopsa, and Mopsa retorts that he has already slept with Dorcas and that she may be pregnant: 'may be he has paid you more, which will shame you to give him again'. The Clown seems to be shocked by their public airing of their differences, and his speech silencing them also contains important information for a director: ''Tis well they are whisp'ring. Clamor your tongues, and not a word more.' As before, with all appearance of honesty, Autolycus warns the Clown against being 'cozened' (cheated or fooled). The Clown reassures him that his property will be safe at their feast.

With a naive faith in the authority of print, Mopsa and Dorcas demand to see ballads: 'I love a ballad in print, a life, for then we are sure they are true.' Autolycus proceeds to tell the outrageous stories of two ballads, more 'tales' to entertain his hearers (designed, like the play itself, to evoke their wonder):

> Here's another ballad, of a fish that appeared upon the coast
> on Wednesday the fourscore of April, forty thousand fathom
> above water, and sung this ballad against the hard hearts of
> maids. It was thought she was a woman, and was turned into
> a cold fish for she would not exchange flesh with one that
> loved her.
> *(lines 260–5)*

When he tells them of a third popular ballad, Mopsa and Dorcas
are keen to sing it. It turns out to be a simple, silly song but one that
offers much opportunity for comedy on stage. Commenting that his
father and the guests are still talking seriously, the Clown leads the
girls and Autolycus off stage, promising to buy gifts for both Mopsa
and Dorcas. Autolycus, clearly determined to fleece him, has the last
words: 'And you shall pay well for 'em.'

The servant announces another entertainment for the feast, a
dance of twelve 'Saltiers' (satyrs – half men, half goats). The Shepherd
is reluctant to weary his guests with more 'homely foolery', but
Polixenes expresses a desire to see the dance. The servant tells him
that 'One three' of the group claims to have danced for the king.
Ironically, now all of them will. Dramatically, this interlude allows
Polixenes to observe the behaviour of his son and Perdita.

After the dancers leave, Polixenes concludes his conversation with
the Shepherd and comments to Camillo that it is time that Florizel
and Perdita are separated. As a preliminary he asks Florizel why he
has not bought gifts for Perdita from the pedlar. Polixenes says that he
used to buy gifts for his love:

> I would have ransacked
> The pedlar's silken treasury and have poured it
> To her acceptance.
> *(lines 328–30)*

Polixenes tells Florizel that Perdita could interpret his not buying
gifts as 'lack of love or bounty' (that he does not love her enough or is
ungenerous). Florizel tells Polixenes that the gift Perdita expects is his
love. He begins to make a public declaration of his love. He uses
conventional courtly praise for the quality of her hand. As a
shepherd's daughter her hand would be roughened by work and

tanned by exposure to outdoor life. Only courtly ladies could keep smooth skin. Again, in this non-naturalistic speech, Shakespeare seems to be suggesting that even the quality of her appearance is conditioned by her royal blood. Polixenes interrupts Florizel's praise of Perdita, which seems to prompt Florizel into making a more explicit and elaborate declaration of his fidelity to Perdita:

> were I crowned the most imperial monarch,
> Thereof most worthy, were I the fairest youth
> That ever made eye swerve, had force and knowledge
> More than was ever man's, I would not prize them
> Without her love; for her employ them all,
> Commend them and condemn them to her service
> Or to their own perdition.   *(lines 351–7)*

Polixenes dryly comments, 'Fairly offered.' Perdita's response to Florizel is less elaborately phrased though just as committed.

>   I cannot speak
> So well, nothing so well; no, nor mean better.
> By th'pattern of mine own thoughts I cut out
> The purity of his.   *(lines 359–62)*

Although on stage this public declaration of their love is often made only to an audience of two strangers, it induces the Shepherd to proclaim their binding betrothal. Ironically he promises to 'make / Her portion equal his', which of course it will eventually. The Shepherd is referring to the gold left with Perdita by Antigonus 'to breed' her – pay for her upbringing. Florizel imagines that, whatever the Shepherd has in mind, it cannot match his wealth and position as heir to the kingdom. As Florizel is aware that the Shepherd does not know his true identity, he merely refers to: 'One being dead, / I shall have more than you can dream of yet'.

As the audience is aware of the identities of all the characters on stage, the series of interruptions by Polixenes that follows serves to heighten both the tension and the potential for comedy. Polixenes asks about Florizel's father, whether he knows of his son's intended marriage, and points out that the bridegroom's father is the most important guest at the wedding of his son. Polixenes asks whether

Florizel's father is so old that he is incapable of reasonable affairs and tells him that his refusal to tell his father is an insult: 'a wrong / Something unfilial'. Polixenes says that a father's interest is in posterity – his descendants. Florizel is insistent that his father must not know, but he refuses to justify his decision. The debate between them gets sharper as their lines become shorter, and the Shepherd eventually feels the need to intervene to support his unknown guest:

> Let him, my son. He shall not need to grieve
> At knowing of thy choice.   *(lines 394–5)*

Florizel continues to refuse: 'Come, come, he must not. / Mark our contract.' Suddenly Polixenes removes his disguise: 'Mark your divorce, young sir'. His action and the line together often provoke laughter in the theatre, partly because the revelation has been expected for some time. It is difficult, however, to laugh at the violence of Polixenes' threats. The instant change of mood is reminiscent of the sudden onset of Leontes' jealousy and his brutal intentions towards Hermione and her baby. Polixenes calls the Shepherd a traitor and promises to have him hanged; he threatens to have Perdita's 'beauty scratched with briars'. He says he will disown Florizel if he shows any regret at losing Perdita. As he leaves, he moderates his threats slightly, reprieving the Shepherd. Though Polixenes warns Perdita that if she ever receives Florizel again she will be cruelly executed, he does seem to value her, saying that she would be worthy of Florizel were he not the prince, who by his deception makes himself unworthy of her:

> And you, enchantment,
> Worthy enough a herdsman – yea, him too
> That makes himself, but for our honour therein,
> Unworthy thee   *(lines 413–16)*

With a final chilling threat to Perdita, Polixenes abruptly leaves the scene. Perdita speaks of being 'not much afeard' and says that she almost spoke to Polixenes to remind him of their common humanity:

> The self-same sun that shines upon his court
> Hides not his visage from our cottage but
> Looks on alike   *(lines 423–5)*

She asks Florizel to leave, reminding him of her earlier fears (lines 35–40). The Shepherd seems not to have heard Polixenes' suspension of the threat of hanging, only his sentence of death. He reproves Florizel and Perdita for their betrayal, and leaves in great distress. Florizel tells Perdita that he is sorry his father has discovered them but that he is neither afraid nor is his love for her changed.

Camillo advises Florizel not to speak to his father until 'the fury of his highness settle'. Only now does Florizel realise that the second stranger is Camillo. Florizel reaffirms his love for and commitment to Perdita, even though she doubts the possibility of their marriage, and Camillo advises him to think again. Florizel uses extravagant imagery to reinforce his vow to Perdita:

> Not for Bohemia, nor the pomp that may
> Be thereat gleaned, for all the sun sees, or
> The close earth wombs, or the profound seas hides
> In unknown fathoms, will I break my oath
> To this my fair beloved.   (lines 467–71)

Florizel says that he does not intend to see his father but that Camillo can tell Polixenes that he has left the country on board his ship, which happens to be conveniently near. Shakespeare organises his characters so that Florizel has something private to say to Perdita, leaving Camillo to deliver a short speech (lines 486–92) that reveals his intentions to the audience. The dilemma faced by Camillo here reminds the audience of his internal debate in Act 1 (Scene 2, lines 351–63). He hopes to be able to use Florizel's escape to assist his return to 'dear Sicilia'.

Camillo reminds Florizel of the services he has performed for Polixenes. He offers to reveal his plans to help Florizel and Perdita escape, and to try to reconcile Polixenes to the match after they have gone. Florizel thinks that this would be some kind of 'miracle'. Camillo's suggestion is that they journey to Sicilia, where Leontes will be happy to receive them. Just as in Act 1 Camillo saved Polixenes from the wrath of Leontes, he now intends to save Florizel from his father's anger. He suggests that Florizel pretend that they are visiting on Polixenes' instructions. Camillo says that a definite plan of action will be better than 'a wild dedication of yourselves / To unpathed waters, undreamed shores'. He feels that the potential problems of an unplanned journey might affect their love. Perdita denies this, and both Camillo and Florizel praise her manner:

> She's as forward of her breeding as
> She is i'th'rear our birth.   *(lines 559–60)*

Florizel raises a practical problem; he does not have the necessary clothes and servants to look as though he is representing Polixenes in Sicilia. Camillo says that he will provide everything as though they were his actors and he were sponsoring their play: 'as if / The scene you play were mine'.

Once again the tone of the scene and the pattern of actors on the stage change as Camillo draws Perdita and Florizel apart to discuss details, and Autolycus comes on stage. He reminds the audience of what was happening when he left the stage as he speaks of the selling of all his goods, which he now terms 'trumpery'. He says that his trinkets were bought as though they were holy relics. This enabled him to see who had most money and, while the Clown was singing, he managed to pick everyone's purse. He is so absorbed in boasting of his skill that he does not notice Camillo, Florizel and Perdita come forward until they speak, and then he worries that he has been overheard, fearing that he will be hanged.

When Camillo sees Autolycus his plan is instantly amended to include an exchange of clothes between Florizel and Autolycus. This offers the actors further opportunity for stage business. Perdita is also instructed by Camillo to disguise herself. Whilst they are occupied, Camillo reveals his plans to the audience in another aside. His intention is to betray the lovers to Polixenes and persuade him to follow them. Camillo will then be able to return with him to Sicilia,

> for whose sight
> I have a woman's longing.   *(lines 635–6)*

As soon as Camillo, Perdita and Florizel have left the stage, Autolycus regains his confidence. He boasts about his 'open ear', 'quick eye' and 'nimble hand'. He is pleased with his new clothes and the money ('boot') that he was paid to make the exchange. He decides that he is being more 'constant' (faithful) to his profession of dishonesty by helping the prince to deceive his father. Autolycus foresees more profit approaching when the Clown and the Shepherd enter: 'more matter for a hot brain'.

The Clown is trying to persuade his father that the way to save his life is to tell Polixenes that Perdita is not his child, and to prove it by showing him all the things that were found with her. The Shepherd agrees, blaming Florizel for intending to make him related to the king. Now wearing the clothes he has received from Florizel, Autolycus accosts the Shepherd and Clown, pretending to be a courtier (a great opportunity for over-acting). They are instantly respectful towards him. Autolycus parodies the insolent and haughty manner of a courtier and demands to know their business, using words that they do not understand. The Clown thinks he knows that 'advocate' means a bribe: 'Advocate's the court-word for a pheasant.' This gives Autolycus the opportunity to invite the audience to be complicit with him in laughing at their ignorance: 'How blest are we that are not simple men!'

The Shepherd seems to have an instinctive mistrust of Autolycus: 'His garments are rich, but he wears them not handsomely.' When the Shepherd says that he must only show the box to the king, Autolycus tells him that the king has gone on board his new ship. He terrifies both the Shepherd and his son by talking of the horrible exaggerated tortures and deaths that will be suffered by the father and brother of the girl who was to have married the prince. Autolycus then offers, for a consideration, to take them to the king and to speak on their behalf. The Shepherd and the Clown are so frightened, 'Remember – "stoned" and "flayed alive"', that they agree to give him gold, and the Shepherd even suggests leaving his son as hostage while he obtains more gold. Autolycus takes what he has been offered and says he will trust them for the rest. Having sent them on ahead, he explains to the audience that he will escort them, not to the king, but to Florizel. Autolycus hopes to do Florizel some good and also to receive a reward:

To him will I present them; there may be matter in it.

(line 780)

Act 4: Critical review

The figure of Time is one of Shakespeare's most innovative devices. Time speaks in rhyming couplets, which some critics used to regard as old-fashioned, leading them to assume that the lines were not written by Shakespeare. However, Time's speech possesses thematic and dramatic complexity. In 16 couplets to represent the 16 years that have passed, Time narrates the course of Leontes' grief and Perdita's maturing 'in grace'. Dramatically, Time's speech draws attention to the fact that the audience is watching a play.

Although the sheep-shearing festival in Act 4 is set in Bohemia, it presents an idealisation of the English countryside, a pastoral Eden which contrasts vividly with the sophisticated Sicilian court. The Clown and the rivals for his affection, Mopsa and Dorcas, represent a contrasting view of rural England. Autolycus, too, exposes the reality of contemporary life. In spite of the disarming way in which he admits his faults to the audience and invites them to join him in laughing at those he is gulling, he is a thief who preys on those who have helped him.

The theme of appearance and reality is evident in the clear stage directions about clothes. Polixenes and Camillo are disguised, Autolycus is in such ragged apparel that even the Clown is shocked, and Perdita is dressed as queen of the sheep-shearing, almost as a goddess.

When Perdita greets the disguised Polixenes and Camillo, her imagery concerns nature and the seasons, emphasising the fertility and plenty of summer. Their debate about nature and art raises one of the major questions of the play, and, though Polixenes appears to win the intellectual argument, Perdita has the final word.

Many critics have commented on the length of time before Polixenes reveals himself. Dramatically, tension is raised by the frequent interruptions of Florizel's declaration of love. The force of Polixenes' anger is shockingly reminiscent of Leontes' fury earlier. Shakespeare ensures that all the essential characters will eventually meet in Sicilia by having the Shepherd and Clown waylaid by Autolycus, who sees them as a potential means of regaining Florizel's favour.

Act 5 Scene 1

The location switches back to Sicilia, where Cleomenes speaks of Leontes' long period of grieving as showing a 'saint-like sorrow'. Leontes feels that he can neither forget Hermione's virtue nor his own contribution to her death and that of Mamillius. Paulina agrees and goes further by suggesting that if he married, one by one, all the women in the world, or from all women alive took their best quality to make a perfect woman, still 'she you killed / Would be unparalleled'. As in Act 3, Paulina is forthright and uncompromising. Cleomenes and Dion wish the king to remarry for the good of the state. They accuse Paulina of not thinking sufficiently of the political consequences:

> You pity not the state nor the remembrance
> Of his most sovereign name; consider little
> What dangers by his highness' fail of issue
> May drop upon his kingdom and devour
> Incertain lookers-on. *(lines 25–9)*

Paulina insists that there is no one good enough, and reminds them of Apollo's oracle. She also speaks of an historical precedent: 'Great Alexander / Left his to th'worthiest'. Leontes says he wishes he had always followed her advice and agrees that there is no woman who is the equal of Hermione. For him to marry a woman who was not Hermione's equal and to treat her more kindly, would cause Hermione's ghost to 'appear soul-vexed / And begin, "Why to me?"'. The image of Hermione's ghost appearing to reproach Leontes if he remarried is a reminder of Antigonus' dream (Act 3 Scene 3, lines 15–45) and it seems to reinforce the idea of Hermione's death. Paulina says that she would encourage the murder of the new wife were she a ghost in Hermione's place, and she reminds Leontes of the beauty of Hermione's eyes. He describes them as

> Stars, stars,
> And all eyes else dead coals! *(lines 67–8)*

Against the protests of Cleomenes, Paulina encourages Leontes to promise 'Never to marry but by my free leave'. She will choose him a wife that would please even Hermione's ghost. He gives his word and

Paulina says he can only marry when Hermione lives again.

A servant arrives to announce the presence of Prince Florizel and his princess with few attendants. Leontes questions the servant, who describes the princess as 'the most peerless piece of earth'. Paulina is quick to point out that the same man had once described Hermione in similar terms. The servant apologises, but also claims that Paulina will agree when she has seen Florizel's princess:

> Women will love her that she is a woman
> More worth than any man; men that she is
> The rarest of all women.   *(lines 110–12)*

Paulina prompts Leontes' guilt by reminding him that there was only a month between the ages of Florizel and Mamillius. Leontes is distressed: 'thou know'st / He dies to me again when talked of'.

When Florizel and Perdita enter, Leontes comments on Florizel's similarity to his father at the same age: 'I should call you brother, / As I did him'. His words are a reminder of the emphasis in Act 1 of the close friendship between Polixenes and Leontes as children and young men. Leontes thinks again of the loss of his son and daughter when he looks at Florizel and Perdita, and he also regrets the loss of Polixenes' friendship. Florizel speaks of his father's greetings to Leontes and he excuses Polixenes' absence by saying he is too ill to travel. Leontes feels again the guilt of his offences against Polixenes, but greets Florizel and Perdita warmly:

> Welcome hither,
> As is the spring to th'earth!   *(lines 150–1)*

Leontes' reference to spring is a reminder of the cycle of the seasons and the promise of spring after winter, also perhaps of the end of the 'sad tale' of winter in Sicilia.

Leontes is surprised that Polixenes has allowed 'this paragon' (Perdita) to visit him, 'a man not worth her pains'. Florizel is forced to invent a background for Perdita: that she is the daughter of a Libyan warlord, an unlikely antecedent that often gets a laugh in performance. Florizel accounts for the small number of his followers by saying that he has sent most of them to Bohemia to announce his successful marriage and safe journey to Sicilia.

Leontes comments on Polixenes' well-deserved good fortune and on his own sins that have led to the loss of his own son and daughter. The mood on stage changes as a lord enters and completes Leontes' line of verse by announcing the arrival of Polixenes and the request that Leontes should arrest Florizel and the Shepherd's daughter with him. The lord also says that Perdita's father and brother have been arrested by Camillo, and he describes their abject fear: 'Never saw I / Wretches so quake.' Leontes questions Florizel, 'Is this the daughter of a king?' and regrets that Florizel has disobeyed his father and chosen a bride 'not so rich in worth as beauty'. Florizel reaffirms his love for Perdita and asks Leontes to speak on their behalf: 'at your request / My father will grant precious things as trifles'. When Leontes says that he would request Perdita, who is not valued by Polixenes ('Which he counts but a trifle'), Paulina is quick to intervene with a rebuke: 'Your eye hath too much youth in't'. Dramatic irony is evident as Leontes justifies himself by saying that he was thinking of Hermione even while he was looking at Perdita. He promises to support Florizel provided that he and Perdita have not slept together: 'Your honour not o'erthrown by your desires'.

Act 5 Scene 2

This scene is unusual in that the majority of the characters are anonymous 'gentlemen', and that most of the scene is the relating of very dramatic events that have happened off stage. Autolycus is the trigger for the explanations. He does not have sufficient status to be present at the events yet is curious to know the outcome of his plotting.

The first Gentleman mentions the 'opening of the fardel' but is unable to tell more because he was asked to leave. His part of the story is to describe the 'passion of wonder' at the meeting between Leontes and Camillo. The second Gentleman reveals the fact that the king's daughter has been found and he declares that the 'ballad-makers cannot be able to express it', which seems ironic after Autolycus' exaggerated ballads in Act 4. The second Gentleman invites the third Gentleman, 'the Lady Paulina's steward', to confirm the story which is 'so like an old tale'.

The third Gentleman makes known the details of what was in the fardel and box brought by the Shepherd. He speaks of the emotional meeting of Leontes and Polixenes; 'their joy waded in tears'. The Gentleman claims that they were so affected by passion that they could only be recognised by their clothes, not by their features. He describes Leontes as being overjoyed at being reunited with Perdita, but also grief-stricken once more at the loss of Hermione. Having described the encounter in detail, the third Gentleman goes on to say it was indescribable.

When asked about the fate of Antigonus, the third Gentleman says it was 'Like an old tale still', and he describes the confused emotions of Paulina, full of grief for her husband and of joy at the fulfilment of the oracle. The first Gentleman uses the image of the theatre when he speaks of both the actors and the audience of these events as kings and princes. The third Gentleman recounts the reaction of Perdita to Leontes' confession of the way in which her mother died, and says that he found this the most touching moment of all and that everyone present found it moving. He tells of the whole court intending to visit the place where Paulina has a statue of Hermione. The second Gentleman says he has noticed that Paulina has visited 'that removed house' two or three times a day since the death of Hermione. All three gentlemen decide to join the court and see the statue for themselves.

The revelations in this scene are very dramatic, and it seems unusual for Shakespeare not to exploit the potential for affecting the feelings of the audience by actually showing the actions the Gentlemen describe. Critics often suggest that the reason Shakespeare uses this 'reporting' style is because he did not want to detract from the dramatic impact of the statue scene.

After the emotional accounts of all the meetings, Shakespeare changes the tone to comedy. Autolycus has stood deferentially listening, but alone on stage regains his confidence. He feels that his part in the revelations would gain him promotion, were he not dedicated to dishonesty. The Shepherd and the Clown come on stage and he comments on their appearance in new clothes: 'in the blossoms of their fortune'.

The Clown now claims to be a 'gentleman born'; even their clothes, he says, are 'gentleman born'. (See pages 65–6 for a longer discussion of Shakespeare's attitude to social class.) Conciliatory now, Autolycus agrees and the Clown says that he has been a 'gentleman born' for four hours and retells the story of the establishment of Perdita's identity from his point of view. Possibly in hopes of reinstatement in the prince's service, Autolycus apologises and asks them to give the prince a good report of him. The Clown says that, now he is a gentleman, he can swear that Autolycus is a brave man and not a drunkard, though he knows Autolycus is a coward and he drinks, because gentlemen can swear to anything for their friends.

Act 5 Scene 3

Leontes and the court are visiting Paulina's home. He thanks her for all the comfort she has given him and asks about the statue of Hermione. Paulina says that, just as Hermione was above every living woman, her statue is better than all the works of art they have seen, therefore she keeps it separate.

Paulina reveals the statue and Shakespeare makes it clear from her words that those who look on the statue are silent in wonder. On stage this is always a tense and dramatic moment. Leontes praises the statue for its likeness to Hermione, commenting on its qualities of tenderness and grace. 'Grace' is a word associated with Hermione and with Perdita throughout the play. Then he notices that the statue represents Hermione as older than he remembers and Polixenes agrees: 'O not by much!' – a line which can get an unfortunate laugh in performance, fracturing the sense of wonder that the scene builds up. Paulina praises the skill of the sculptor in being able to make Hermione's statue appear 16 years older and make her look 'As she lived now'. Leontes is deeply moved by the appearance of the statue; he remembers wooing Hermione and feels renewed shame.

Leontes and Perdita both speak of its 'magic' qualities. Perdita wishes to ask the blessing of the statue, but thinks that she will be censured for superstition. She wishes to kiss the statue's hand but Paulina stops her, saying that the paint is not yet dry. Shakespeare makes Leontes' emotional reactions clear through the comments of Camillo, Polixenes and Paulina, who all try to comfort him. Leontes stops Paulina from drawing the curtain across the statue and comments again on its life-like qualities, asking Polixenes:

> See, my lord,
> Would you not deem it breathed, and that those veins
> Did verily bear blood? *(lines 63–5)*

Polixenes agrees, but again Paulina says she will draw the curtain before Leontes' mind becomes affected so much that he believes that the statue lives. Leontes says that he prefers the madness that thinks so to sanity. Paulina apologises for having affected his emotions so profoundly but claims that she could 'afflict' him further. Leontes uses her word in reply: 'this affliction has a taste as sweet / As any cordial comfort'. He is convinced that the statue breathes and moves to kiss it. Paulina reminds him that the paint is still wet, and for the third time offers to draw the curtain across the statue. Both Leontes and Perdita claim that they could look at the statue 'these twenty years'.

Paulina raises the emotional tension by giving them a choice; either they leave the chapel or they should prepare themselves for a further surprise. This is the first time that Shakespeare has made it explicit that the scene suggests an action in a chapel and it is perhaps relevant that this reference is in a speech where Paulina denies that she is 'assisted / By wicked powers'. Leontes gives permission and Paulina asks those present to 'awake your faith'. She calls for music and gives a series of instructions to the statue:

> 'Tis time; descend; be stone no more; approach;
> Strike all that look upon with marvel. Come;
> I'll fill your grave up. Stir; nay, come away;
> Bequeath to death your numbness, for from him
> Dear life redeems you.   *(lines 99–103)*

When the statue begins to stir, Paulina emphasises that Hermione's actions are 'holy' and that her own spell is 'lawful'. Leontes does not at first move towards Hermione and has to be prompted by Paulina to take her hand. Leontes' first words, 'O, she's warm!', are poignant and they give a sense of emotional realism to the moment. Shakespeare gives the stage directions to the other characters as Hermione and Leontes embrace, unspeaking. It is Polixenes who asks Paulina where Hermione has been living and how she is alive. Paulina tells him that if he had only heard an announcement that she was alive he would dismiss the report as 'an old tale' and she tells him just to observe.

Paulina then encourages Perdita to kneel to receive Hermione's blessing, and Hermione turns to her daughter:

> You gods, look down,
> And from your sacred vials pour your graces
> Upon my daughter's head!   *(lines 121–3)*

Hermione questions Perdita about where she has lived, and she claims to have kept herself alive in order to see her:

> Knowing by Paulina that the oracle
> Gave hope thou wast in being, have preserved
> Myself to see the issue.   *(lines 126–8)*

Hermione's blessing and her unanswered questions are her only lines in this part of the play. She says nothing to Leontes and this presents a challenge to directors. Many assume that the fact that she has embraced Leontes ('She hangs about his neck', line 112) means that there is reconciliation. A few directors take a darker view. One production left Hermione and Perdita silent together on stage at the end of the play.

For the last time, Paulina directs the action, stopping all questions and asking them to leave: 'your exultation / Partake to every one'. She compares herself to an old turtledove, conventionally supposed to mate for life, who will grieve for her lost husband.

The reconciliation of Leontes and Hermione is usually a magical and emotional moment in the theatre. As in the other late plays, Shakespeare emphasises the regenerative power of repentance and forgiveness. (See pages 53–5 for more on Shakespeare's late plays.) Leontes now takes charge and speaks the final lines of the play. He reminds Paulina that as he had promised that he would only marry with her consent, she must now take a husband by his. Leontes chooses Camillo, suggesting that 'I partly know his mind'. Neither Camillo nor Paulina has any lines to show their reaction but the pairing of important characters is a conventional ending to a comedy. Though some directors choose to suggest that this is not a happy solution, most suggest that it is joyful. Leontes notices that Hermione will not look at Polixenes, and apologises again to each of them for his suspicions. Leontes also presents Florizel to Hermione and asks Paulina to lead everyone away to resolve all questions off stage,

> where we may leisurely
> Each one demand and answer to his part
> Performed in this wide gap of time since first
> We were dissevered.   *(lines 152–5)*

Act 5: Critical review

The action returns to Sicilia, where Leontes is praised by his courtiers for his 16 years' 'saint-like sorrow' for the dead Hermione. Paulina remains forthright. She defies the courtiers and reminds Leontes strongly of what he has done, as though she were the voice of his conscience: 'she you killed'. From the courtiers' point of view the urgent pressure is on Leontes to provide the kingdom with an heir; they wish him to remarry. The announcement of the arrival of the son of Polixenes breaks into the argument just as Paulina has made Leontes promise never to marry without her permission. When Leontes greets Florizel and Perdita with 'Welcome hither, / As is the spring to th'earth!', it seems a hint that the winter of grief in Sicilia is nearly over.

Scene 2 has troubled many critics who feel cheated of the drama of the meeting of Leontes with the friend he suspected of seducing his wife, and the revelation that Perdita is his daughter. No one knows why Shakespeare chose this daring way of telling this part of the story, but many feel that it was to ensure that it does not detract from a strong emotional and dramatic focus on the statue scene. After the moving description of the family meetings, it is parodied by the comic reconciliation of Autolycus and the men he has cheated. Now that they are 'gentlemen born', they will sponsor him at court.

Shakespeare deliberately builds dramatic tension towards the magical revelation of Hermione that follows in the final scene. He ensures that there is a strong atmosphere of wonder and reverence in the moments leading to the first movement of the statue. Though modern scepticism frequently influences modern productions, for the majority of audiences it is an emotional experience.

There is a poignant simplicity in Leontes' words when he first touches the hand of Hermione, 'O, she's warm!' Shakespeare gives clear stage directions to Hermione in the script, and the embrace of Hermione and Leontes described by Polixenes and Camillo suggests reconciliation and forgiveness. The fortuitous pairing of Camillo and Paulina is sometimes interpreted as offering a humorous release of dramatic tension, allowing the audience to feel joyful rather than overwhelmed by emotion.

Contexts

There is a romantic idea amongst some critics that at the end of his writing life Shakespeare became more serene; that he could no longer cope with the stress of writing tragedies and turned to writing charming romances. It is possible to interpret *The Winter's Tale* in that light, but only by ignoring its complexities and dramatic passion. This section identifies the contexts from which *The Winter's Tale* emerged: the wide range of different influences which fostered the creativity of Shakespeare as he wrote the play. These contexts ensured that *The Winter's Tale* is full of reminders of everyday life, and the familiar knowledge, assumptions, beliefs and values of Jacobean England.

What did Shakespeare write?

Many of Shakespeare's plays were first published as individual quarto books before being collected seven years after his death into the First Folio edition (a quarto is about the size of this page you are reading; a folio page is over twice as large). *The Winter's Tale* does not exist as a quarto; the version in the First Folio is the only original text of the play.

The Winter's Tale was probably written early in 1611 because there is an account of the play in Simon Forman's notes for 15 May of that year. He describes seeing the play at the Globe and tells the story in some detail. He was particularly struck by Autolycus:

> Remember also the Rog (rogue) that cam in all tottered like coll pixci, and howe he fayned him sicke & to have bin robbed of all that he had and howe he cosoned the por man of all his money, and after came to the shep sher with a pedler's packe & ther cosoned them Again of all their money And howe he changed apparrell with the kinge of Bo[he]mia his sonn, and then how he turned Courtier &c.

Because Forman does not mention the statue scene, some critics have suggested that in the first acted versions of the play Hermione remains dead, as in the source story, *Pandosto* (see page 55 below). However there is no evidence to support this, and Forman was probably concentrating on what he perceived as the message of the play: 'Beware of trustinge feined beggars or fawninge felouss'.

It has been suggested that the play was written after the beginning of 1611 because on 1 January of that year there was a masque at court in which a dance of twelve satyrs was performed. In Act 4 Scene 4 of *The Winter's Tale*, the servant announces the dance of the twelve satyrs and says 'One three of them, by their own report, sir, hath danced before the king'. Some critics suggest that this is a contemporary reference to this masque.

The First Folio, containing 36 plays, was published in 1623. These plays had been collected and classified by two members of Shakespeare's company, Heminges and Condell. They are divided into Comedies, Tragedies and Histories. In the Folio, *The Winter's Tale* and *The Tempest* are classified as comedies, *Cymbeline* as a tragedy, and *Pericles* was not included at all. It is only relatively recently that critics have considered that these four late plays share so many features that they should be reclassified as a separate group, either as tragicomedies or romances.

Today, all editions of *The Winter's Tale* are based on that 1623 version, but the edition of the play you are using will vary in many minor respects from other editions. That is because although every editor of the play uses the Folio version, each one makes a multitude of different judgements about such matters as spelling, punctuation, stage directions, scene locations and other features.

So the text of *The Winter's Tale* is not as stable as you might think. This is no reason for dismay, but rather an opportunity to think about how the differences reflect what actually happens in performance. Every production, on stage or film, cuts, adapts and amends the text to present its own unique version of *The Winter's Tale*. This Guide follows the New Cambridge edition of the play (also used in Cambridge School Shakespeare).

The late plays

The four plays written by Shakespeare towards the end of his writing career are *Pericles*, *The Winter's Tale*, *Cymbeline* and *The Tempest*. They share certain characteristics, which leads critics to look at the ways in which the study of all four can illuminate the reading of each single one. This categorisation can also lead to potentially dubious biographical extrapolations, such as that made by H B Charlton, who asserts that in old age Shakespeare wrote the plays to cheer himself in the face of the pain and suffering that humans endure: 'an old man's consolation for the harshness of man's lot'. The late plays display linguistic similarities. Many of the images are repeated, and in each play Shakespeare uses blank verse with poetic vividness. There are more shared lines than in nearly all the earlier plays. They share certain elements of plot and theme:

- a three-part structure, with a potentially tragic opening, a long period of time for growth and learning, and a final resolution which does not depend entirely on the actions of the characters but on magic or chance (in *The Tempest* the first two parts take place before the play opens and their action is narrated by Prospero)
- the breakdown of a close relationship
- a lost child who is found again
- a daughter who is closely identified with the themes of regeneration and rebirth
- a questioning of the relationship between nature and nurture
- a concern with the chastity of women
- shipwrecks and storms
- magic, myth, fairy-tale and folklore – all of which create a sense of wonder
- a final reconciliation which suggests hope for restoration and renewal

The Winter's Tale has all the characteristics of the late plays, but it is unusual for several reasons. In no other play does Shakespeare keep secret from the audience such an important element of the plot as the restoration of Hermione. If you think of *Romeo and Juliet*, the audience knows what is going to happen as soon as they have heard the prologue. In all the tragedies, every stage of the action is revealed to the audience (even if critics disagree about the interpretation). In the comedies, the audience almost always knows more than the characters. Only once, in an early play, *The Comedy of Errors*, does Shakespeare reveal to the characters and the audience together that a woman, Emilia, previously thought dead is actually alive. However, in *The Comedy of Errors* this is only the last in a long line of improbable coincidences and Emilia has had no other part in the action.

Another unusual feature of *The Winter's Tale* is that Mamillius,

Antigonus and the mariners all die. In *The Tempest*, for example, though there is a fierce storm and the ship appears wrecked, it has all been part of the illusion created by Prospero and Ariel. The main characters land in different parts of Prospero's island, each group thinking that they are the only survivors, and the mariners join them at the end of the play saying that their ship is 'tight and yare and bravely rigged as when / We first put out to sea'. In *Pericles* there is also a storm and Thaisa, Pericles' wife, is thought dead by both Pericles and the audience. Her coffin is thrown overboard, but the audience witnesses the finding of the coffin and the restoration of Thaisa. In *Cymbeline* the only major character to die is Cloten, and he is not a sympathetic character. In *The Winter's Tale* there seems less emphasis on reconciling all the various elements of the story, and thus perhaps a more muted joy; Antigonus and Mamillius, the child 'of the greatest promise', remain sacrifices to Leontes' jealous delusions and tyranny.

The *Winter's Tale* also differs from the other late plays in the way that it is structured. In *Pericles* and *Cymbeline* the tragic and comic elements of the play are more intertwined, and in *The Tempest* the potentially tragic episodes have taken place before the play opens and they are related to Miranda by her father during Act 1. Only in *The Winter's Tale* is there such a marked division structurally between the tragic events of the first three acts and the restoration of harmony in the later acts. Unique also to *The Winter's Tale* is the intense emotion and grief associated with the tragic element of the play.

What did Shakespeare read?

Apart from taking material from Ovid's *Metamorphoses*, which he had often used before, and from one or two other minor sources, Shakespeare took the main plot of *The Winter's Tale* from a story by Robert Greene, called *Pandosto*. There is a certain irony in the fact that one of Shakespeare's greatest plays is based on a story written by a university writer who gave him an early bad review, calling him 'an upstart crow, beautified with our feathers'. There was great jealousy felt by those playwrights who had had a more extended classical education at Oxford or Cambridge towards those like Shakespeare who had learned their craft more practically; in Shakespeare's case by also being an actor. Greene's prose story, *Pandosto* or *The Triumph of Time*, was published in 1588 and reprinted three times during

Shakespeare's lifetime. It was evidently very popular. There are many similarities between *Pandosto* and *The Winter's Tale*, even extending to phrases taken straight from the story, which suggests either that Shakespeare was working with a copy of the story in front of him, or that he had an unusually good ear for a turn of phrase. The following summary includes a number of examples of Greene's phrases:

In *Pandosto*, which is sub-titled *The History of Dorastus and Fawnia*, Pandosto is King of Bohemia. His wife is called Bellaria and their son, Garinter; 'the perfection of the child greatly augmented the love of the parents and the joy of their commons'. They were visited by Egistus, King of Sicilia, who was 'desirous to shew that neither tract of time nor distance of place could diminish their former friendship'. Bellaria was 'willing to shew how unfeignedly she loved her husband by his friend's entertainment, oftentimes coming herself into his bedchamber to see that nothing should be amiss to mislike him'. Pandosto 'grew at last to a flaming jealousy that so tormented him as he could take no rest'. He was determined to poison Egistus and tried to bribe his cupbearer, Franion, to do this. Franion tried to dissuade Pandosto but eventually said that he would. Alone, Franion meditates on the reasons why he should not kill Egistus and decides to warn him instead. They flee through the postern gates of the city. Pandosto is furious and has Bellaria arrested while she is playing with her young son. Bellaria 'finding her clear conscience a sure advocate to plead in her case, went to the prison most willingly'. Pandosto 'caused a general proclamation to be made through all his realm that the queen and Egistus had, by the help of Franion, not only committed most incestuous adultery, but also had conspired the king's death'.

When Bellaria's daughter was born in prison Pandosto 'determined that both Bellaria and the young infant should be burnt with fire'. Pandosto's nobles pleaded with him and he decided to have the child set adrift from an open boat. Bellaria wept when the child was taken from her and put a chain around the child's neck. Bellaria begged Pandosto to send to the oracle of Apollo at Delphos; if the oracle said she was guilty she would be content to suffer anything. Pandosto agreed. The sealed message from the oracle said: 'Suspicion is no proof: Jealousy is an unequal judge: Bellaria is chaste: Egistus blameless: Franion a true subject: Pandosto treacherous: his babe an innocent; and the king shall live without an heir, if that which is lost be not found'. Pandosto is immediately shamed and intends to seek reconciliation with Bellaria and Egistus when news is brought of the death of his son Garinter. Bellaria hears the news and dies. Egistus buries Bellaria and her son together, and he visits the tomb once a day, weeping.

'But leaving him to his dolorous passions, at last let us come to shew the tragical discourse of the young infant.' She is found by a shepherd, Porrus, who is looking for a missing sheep by the seaside. He finds a purse of gold with the child and takes both to his wife, Mopsa. They call the child Fawnia and: 'she so increased in exquisite perfection both of body and mind . . . she seemed to be the goddess Flora herself for beauty'. The fame of her beauty spreads to court where Egistus is angry with his son, Dorastus, for not wishing to marry yet. Whilst out hawking Dorastus comes across Fawnia dressed as mistress of a feast for farmers' daughters. They fall in love. Dorastus feels that it is wrong for him to love a shepherd's daughter and resolves not to see her again. Fawnia realises that there is no future in their love, and tries to forget him. However they meet again while Dorastus is hawking and he talks with her and realises that she is as virtuous and wise as she is beautiful. She says that she will only love him when he becomes a shepherd. Dorastus considers that the gods have transformed themselves for love: 'Neptune became a ram, Jupiter a bull, Apollo a shepherd', and he dresses as a shepherd.

Dorastus and Fawnia decide to run away together as soon as Dorastus can gather sufficient treasure. Neighbours warn Porrus that Dorastus seems to be attracted to his daughter. As he has no wish to displease the King or his son, Porrus decides to tell the King that Fawnia is not his daughter. His wife agrees and makes her husband tidy for the king. She 'sponged him up very handsomely, giving him the chain and the jewels in a little box'. On his way the shepherd meets Capnio, the servant of Dorastus, hurrying towards the prince's ship with his treasure. Capnio takes the shepherd forcibly on board.

The ship lands in Bohemia. Dorastus is afraid that Pandosto will kill him because he is the son of Egistus so he changes his name. Pandosto falls in love with Fawnia and accuses Dorastus of stealing a great lady from her parents. He throws Dorastus in prison and tries to seduce Fawnia, but she resists him. He threatens to take her by force. Messengers from Egistus beg Pandosto to arrest Fawnia, Porrus and Capnio, but to treat his son well for his sake. Pandosto condemns Fawnia and Porrus to death: 'how durst thou presume, being a beggar, to match with a prince?' He says that Capnio will have his eyes put out and spend the rest of his life in a mill, turning the wheel like an animal. In defence Porrus shows the little box which contains Bellaria's chain and tells how he found the baby. Pandosto is overjoyed that his daughter has been found and the 'citizens and subjects of Bohemia . . . made bonfires'. Pandosto makes Porrus a knight and journeys with Fawnia and Dorastus to Sicilia to visit Egistus and be reconciled to him. Once Fawnia and Dorastus are married, Pandosto considers all his faults; his betrayal of Egistus, his jealousy of Bellaria, his lusting after his own daughter, and he kills himself. Everyone else lives happily ever after.

It is illuminating to consider the major changes that Shakespeare made to Greene's story. The similarities are clear and the minor changes, such as the transposition of Bohemia and Sicilia (Greene evidently also thought that Bohemia had a sea-coast) are of little importance. Shakespeare also changed the names of the characters, using many with classical associations (and significantly re-naming Fawnia 'Perdita', the lost one). It is the way that Shakespeare used and developed the source story that merits detailed consideration. In *Pandosto* there is much more emphasis on the role of fortune in the lives of the characters. In *The Winter's Tale*, humans bear all the responsibility. Leontes shows pride and arrogance in his rejection of the message from Apollo's oracle, Camillo organises the escapes from and to Sicilia, Hermione 'preserves' herself to await the restoration of her daughter. Though there are many elements of myth and fairy-tale, the major events in *The Winter's Tale* are the result of human action.

Shakespeare's main additions to the action of the play are as follows:

- Leontes' jealousy, which is immediate and all-consuming. In *Pandosto*, Pandosto's jealousy is motivated by elements of Bellaria's behaviour such as her visits to Egistus' bedchamber, and it develops over time.
- Antigonus and Paulina are entirely Shakespeare's addition to the story having no parallel in *Pandosto*. Antigonus shows support for his wife even when she defies the king, and dramatically it is Leontes who is isolated in the argument on stage, not Paulina. Antigonus risks being made to look the commonplace figure of fun of Medieval and Renaissance literature – the man who cannot control his own wife. However, Shakespeare ensures that he can be performed to display dignity, and he shows good judgement in his reaction to Paulina:

  > When she will take the rein, I let her run;
  > But she'll not stumble.   *(Act 2 Scene 3, lines 51–2)*

  Paulina is unique amongst the female characters in Shakespeare's comedies in that she organises much of the action without being the central character. She is a mature woman and is not punished or destroyed for her interference. She appears to assume the place at court vacated by Camillo, and it is unusual for a woman to be a close adviser to a king.
- The death of Antigonus is Shakespeare's addition. As Sir Arthur Quiller-Couch asked in the introduction to his edition of *The Winter's Tale*: 'Why introduce a bear?' In *Pandosto*, the child is set adrift in an open boat. Having introduced Antigonus as the instrument of Leontes' tyrannical behaviour, Shakespeare does not include him in the fate of the mariners but reserves an especially gruesome death for him. Critics searching for Shakespeare's motivation have suggested that this is partly so that the Clown can find out Antigonus' name and return his 'handkerchief and rings' to Paulina, thus confirming the identity of Perdita, and partly to effect the change of tone to comedy in the Clown's account of his

death: 'nor the bear half dined on the gentleman'. Other critics
have suggested that the bear is a traditional figure of folklore and
intensifies the atmosphere of Romance.

- The figure of Time marks the 16-year gap in time. In *Pandosto* the
story of the maturing of Perdita is told in the narrative in much
more detail. The action of each of Shakespeare's late plays covers a
substantial amount of time, sufficient in three of the plays for an
infant to grow to marriageable age (in *The Tempest*, that time is
covered by Prospero's narration). Shakespeare's presentation of
Time is important dramatically and thematically. Dramatically, the
narrative of Time at the start of Act 4 takes the audience straight to
the next key moment in the story; Florizel and Perdita are in love,
and barely has this been established in the dramatic action when
adversity strikes them. Thematically, Time leads to the revelation of
the truth:

> I that please some, try all, both joy and terror
> Of good and bad, that makes and unfolds error,
> Now take upon me, in the name of Time,
> To use my wings.   *(Act 4 Scene 1, lines 1–4)*

- Autolycus is possibly Shakespeare's most inventive addition to his
source material as there is no real need for him in the development
of the plot. Shakespeare's intentions therefore are much more
likely to have been to change the dramatic mood of the play.
Autolycus is a great comic creation. He enters singing, reminding
the audience of the changing seasons. He dispels the atmosphere
of disease and excessive emotion prevalent in the first half of the
play. He is cheerfully dishonest, and his down-to-earth
opportunism is in sharp contrast to the intensity of the scenes in
the first part of the play. He adds greatly to the atmosphere of
freshness and vitality in Act 4 Scene 4.

- The nature versus art debate between Polixenes and Perdita in Act
4 Scene 4 is not a particularly original discussion. The subject
would have been discussed widely in Shakespeare's day. The point
to consider is why Shakespeare thought it sufficiently important to
insert it into the sheep-shearing festival, changing the tone of the
original story. In Act 4 Scene 4, Polixenes argues for selective
breeding: 'we marry / A gentler scion to the wildest stock, / And

make conceive a bark of baser kind / By bud of nobler race'. As many critics have pointed out, he is arguing against his own case when speaking to the girl to whom his son is showing affection. Perdita is also arguing against her own interests, though she shifts her ground at the close of the argument, equating art with artificiality. Perhaps Shakespeare is pointing out that there is a world of difference between an abstract intellectual theory and what Polixenes wants in practice for his own son. A prince would not marry a shepherdess. (See also pages 65–6 for more on Jacobean social class.)

- The living statue of Hermione and the reconciliation scene are Shakespeare's most radical departures from his source story. There is only a hint of Leontes' potentially incestuous desire for his own daughter which forms the motive for Pandosto's suicide, and that is almost justified by Leontes' saying, 'I thought of her / Even in these looks I made.' Shakespeare ensures that Leontes does not continue to commit the terrible sins perpetrated by Pandosto; in Greene's story, not only does Pandosto desire Fawnia, but when she refuses him he threatens her with the same kind of violence which had marked his behaviour years before to Bellaria. (Shakespeare transfers these violent threats to Polixenes when he discovers that Florizel intends to marry Perdita.) In *The Winter's Tale*, Leontes seems to have truly repented and he offers to speak in defence of the marriage of Florizel and Perdita. The way is clear for a joyful reconciliation with Hermione. In the theatre, the movement of the statue for the first time is always emotionally thrilling and is an example of Shakespeare's dramatic expertise in influencing the emotional response of his audience.

Pastoral

Shakespeare uses elements of the literary device of pastoral in *The Winter's Tale* and juxtaposes them with a more robust presentation of country life. Pastoral in literature and in art was developed by poets in Ancient Greece who would almost certainly have been studied by Shakespeare in his education at the grammar school in Stratford. The themes of pastoral literature include the evocation of an idealised, noble, yet unsophisticated life lived by peasants, especially shepherds, in an uncorrupted countryside. In Latin 'pastor' means shepherd. As a genre, pastoral frequently merges with romance to give a kind of moral fairy-tale. The best known examples of the pastoral romance are Sir Philip Sydney's *Arcadia* (1590) and Sir Edmund Spenser's *The Faerie Queen* (1596). Shakespeare uses the genre in Act 4 Scene 4 in his presentation of Perdita and Florizel (his idealised shepherdess and shepherd are really a princess and a prince) but contrasts it with recognisable, contemporary rustic characters.

What was Shakespeare's England like?

Although *The Winter's Tale* is set in pre-Christian times and the presiding deity is Apollo, the reality of the play is Jacobean England. Leontes' reference to 'a plot against my life, my crown' could have been seen as a reference to the conspiracies against James I, particularly perhaps the Gunpowder Plot. There are also references to a common toy of the time, 'a schoolboy's top'. Hermione's guilt is published by 'proclamations' seen by Cleomenes and Dion on their way back from Delphi. The proclamation was a common way of making announcements in Jacobean England, as was the use of the post outside the sheriffs' houses referred to by Hermione at her trial: 'Myself on every post / Proclaimed a strumpet'.

The audience going to see *The Winter's Tale* at the Globe would have passed the bear-baiting pit where dogs were set to fight a bear and wagers were placed on the outcome. Some critics have suggested that the bear that chases Antigonus off stage in Act 3 was a pensioned-off bear from the bear-baiting, though this is unlikely given the unpredictability of behaviour on stage of even so-called tame bears.

It is particularly in Act 4 that the audience would recognise contemporary English festivities in the sheep-shearing festival, Perdita's list of common garden flowers and her talk of 'Whitsun pastorals'. Whit Sunday is a festival observed on the seventh Sunday after Easter, commemorating the descent of the Holy Spirit to the Apostles. In Elizabethan and Jacobean England, Whitsun was a time for lively festivals which would involve drinking, dancing and singing. Traditionally, boys would give gifts of ribbons or gloves to their girls.

Autolycus would be a recognisable figure both as a ballad-seller and a pedlar. His pack is full of the kind of goods which would have been sold by any ambitious pedlar of the time. He claims to have once been in the service of Prince Florizel and to have worn 'three-pile' or the most expensive kind of velvet with the pattern cut into the pile, though now he is in rags. Autolycus' ballads were the equivalent of the tabloid press for the country peasants, songs that told of the news and wonders of the day. They appealed to the Jacobean love of wonders; a woman giving birth to twenty money-bags would certainly be a wonder.

But a Jacobean audience would have seen a darker aspect to Autolycus' character. The figure of Autolycus, as a man without a master or trade (except stealing), was feared by the authorities. Such 'masterless' men posed a serious threat to public order. Though Shakespeare presents him entertainingly, Autolycus' references to the kind of punishments he could expect if he is caught are quite chilling: 'Beating and hanging are terrors to me' (Act 4 Scene 3, line 28). The laws dealing with stealing and vagrancy at this time were very severe; those caught begging would be whipped and put in the stocks.

The food that the Clown speaks about buying for the feast is a mark of the rising fortunes of the Shepherd, described by Polixenes as having 'grown into an unspeakable estate'. His flock now numbers fifteen hundred, a very large flock for the time. The practice of enclosing common land for the grazing of sheep and cattle had made a great difference in wealth to those who could afford to do it. In contrast, those who owned a few sheep, which formerly had grazed on common land, became even poorer. Some of Shakespeare's own income in his later life came from enclosures. Jacobean audiences would have recognised the newly wealthy Shepherd as a familiar figure.

The Clown describes the shopping list given to him by Perdita: 'my father hath made her mistress of the feast, and she lays it on'. The festive ingredients show how the Jacobean marketplace was changing, with imported goods and luxury foods being more widely available. He is to buy expensive 'sugar' (when the common sweetener would have been honey), 'currants' and 'rice', all imported foods. Certainly Shakespeare's audience would have recognised that this was an unusually luxurious sheep-shearing festival, a testament to the Shepherd's great wealth.

In yet another contemporary reference, the Clown also makes an ironic mention of a Puritan amongst the shearers who 'sings psalms to hornpipes'. As the Puritans tended to be rather serious and to disapprove of hedonistic enjoyment (and the theatre), this would have been a topical joke to theatre-goers at the time. Whitsun and Christmas were two of the festivals banned by the Puritans when they came to power during the English Civil War. They also closed all theatres. It is not the first time that Shakespeare has made fun of

Puritans: in *Twelfth Night*, Malvolio is humiliated by the pleasure-loving Sir Toby Belch.

When the quarrel between Mopsa and Dorcas threatens to disrupt the festivities, the Clown rebukes them with references to contemporary clothes and farming manners:

> Is there no manners left among maids? Will they wear their
> plackets where they should bear their faces? Is there not
> milking-time, when you are going to bed, or kill-hole, to
> whistle of these secrets   *(Act 4 Scene 4, lines 231–4)*

Plackets were the gaps in women's skirts where they were fastened. These gaps were frequently referred to in plays as having potentially obscene uses, so the Clown is warning Mopsa and Dorcas to keep their language clean. Traditionally, milking-time and during the wait at the baking kiln (kill-hole) were two of the times for a good gossip.

During Shakespeare's time there was strong identification between the state and the throne. Calling the King of Sicilia simply 'Sicilia' was more than just a linguistic convention; the power of kings at this time was so strong that the behaviour and attitude of the king affected the whole country. In Act 5, when Cleomenes and Dion are trying to persuade Leontes to marry again to produce an heir for the benefit of the state, the reference made by Paulina to Alexander would have been recognised by many of those in Shakespeare's audience as relevant to their own time. Queen Elizabeth I had been frequently urged to marry and to have children to prevent strife after her death. After the turmoil of the Wars of the Roses and the threat of civil war after the death of Edward VI, the ordinary people had naturally been concerned about the fate of England if Elizabeth died without an heir. She left her throne to James VI of Scotland (who succeeded as James I of England) and Paulina's lines could therefore have been interpreted as a compliment to King James:

> Great Alexander
> Left his to th'worthiest; so his successor
> Was like to be the best.   *(Act 5 Scene 1, lines 47–9)*

There may also have been a more satirical reference to King James in both the Clown and Shepherd becoming so ridiculously 'gentlemen born': James I was frequently criticised in his own time for creating many new knights.

Critics sometimes suggest that the singing and dancing in Act 4 Scene 4 in some ways parody a court masque. The masque was a courtly form of entertainment where the participants were usually of the same class as the audience. Queen Anne was particularly fond of masques and occasionally performed in them with her ladies. Given that *The Winter's Tale* was performed at court more than once, this could be said to offer a topical compliment to the king and queen.

Some critics think that Shakespeare may have been making an ironic point by choosing Giulio Romano as the painter of Hermione's sculpture, but most feel that he chose a well-known artist to add realism to the scene. Giulio (Julio) Romano was an artist who lived in Italy between 1499 and 1546. He was better known for architecture and painting than sculpture, and particularly his very explicit erotic etchings, which were considered so obscene that they were confined to the Vatican library under lock and key.

All the above examples show how *The Winter's Tale* reflects aspects of Shakespeare's time. What now follows are other significant ways in which the play reveals its context: the structure, culture and beliefs of Jacobean England.

Jacobean social structure

The demarcation between classes was beginning to blur during Shakespeare's time with the increase in wealth and power of the merchant classes. Many farmers and landowners had significantly increased their income by enclosing common land. However, in spite of all such social changes it would still have been unheard of for a prince to marry a real shepherdess. In Act 4, when Florizel seems about to make a declaration of betrothal before witnesses, Polixenes becomes incensed. His extreme reaction implies that Florizel's association with Perdita could perhaps have been tolerated provided it had nothing to do with marriage.

The relationship between nobility of character and high social status had been a subject for discussion since before Chaucer's time. In *The Winter's Tale*, Shakespeare seems to be suggesting that culture and virtue are innate. Though raised from infancy by a shepherd, Perdita can speak in elaborate verse and possesses detailed knowledge of classical literature. She behaves with the courtesy of a princess, and her diction and imagery contrast sharply with those of the Shepherd and Clown. On the other hand, Shakespeare makes it clear that generosity and compassion are not confined to members of the nobility. The Shepherd shows real humanity in his care for the baby he finds by the shore, even though he assumes that it is the result of an illicit liaison: 'I'll take it up for pity'. The Clown is the butt of much humour in the play but he is also kindly and charitable. He offers to go back and bury Antigonus, he plays the Good Samaritan role with Autolycus, and he offers to buy presents for each of his mistresses.

Polixenes does not transfer his theories about grafting, 'A gentler scion to the wildest stock', to his own family. He considers that Perdita is merely 'Worthy enough a herdsman', even though he recognises her special qualities:

> Nothing she does or seems
> But smacks of something greater than herself,
> Too noble for this place. *(Act 4 Scene 4, lines 157–9)*

In *The Winter's Tale*, Shakespeare contributes to the on-going intellectual debate about nature and nurture without trying to give a definitive answer.

Patriarchal authority in Jacobean England

In many ways, the roles of the women in *The Winter's Tale* reflect the attitudes to women current in Shakespeare's day. Women were considered inferior beings, ruled by passion and needing to be controlled by men. They were thought of as the weaker sex, not just physically but weak in self-control. A wife was generally seen as an ornament to her husband if she was virtuous. In plays of the time, women who set up their own opinions against their husbands were frequently presented as adulterous, as if independence were synonymous with unchastity. Once Hermione succeeds in persuading Polixenes to stay, Leontes, who had failed, assumes there is another motive for Polixenes' submission to her will.

The view of women as male possessions was commonplace. It finds sharp expression in *The Taming of the Shrew*. Just after Petruchio has married Kate, his words (based on Exodus 20:17) reflect in brutal terms the attitude of some men at the time to their wives:

I will be master of what is mine own.
She is my goods, my chattels; she is my house,
My household-stuff, my field, my barn,
My horse, my ox, my ass, my anything.

(Act 3 Scene 2, lines 218–21)

A similar attitude emerges in *The Winter's Tale*, where it is firmly linked to male sexual anxiety. Elizabethan and Jacobean men feared women's control over their own bodies, and their potential for opening them to others. Early in the play, Leontes speaks of his love for Hermione, and of his desire for her before she would agree to marry him, in terms which imply her chastity:

Why, that was when
Three crabbèd months had soured themselves to death
Ere I could make thee open thy white hand
And clap thyself my love   *(Act 1 Scene 2, lines 101–4)*

But once he suspects her of adultery, Leontes speaks of Hermione bitterly, as though she were his fishpond or his estate:

Nay, there's comfort in't
Whiles other men have gates, and those gates opened,
As mine, against their will.   *(Act 1 Scene 2, lines 196–8)*

Perdita is also representative of contemporary ideas about young women. She is intelligent but always acknowledges Florizel as her superior. She is called a witch when Polixenes feels she has transgressed the rules governing social class and entrapped his son: 'fresh piece / Of excellent witchcraft'. When she is recognised as a princess, her freedom to express herself is curtailed and she speaks only a few lines more.

Paulina encapsulates several elements of the traditional stock roles for women, the scold, the virago and the witch, but Shakespeare goes far beyond such conventional portrayals with the character of Paulina. Her first words suggest authority:

The keeper of the prison, call to him.
Let him have knowledge who I am.   *(Act 2 Scene 2, lines 1–2)*

The reactions of other characters in the play add to the impression that she is a forceful woman. Even Leontes is wary of her:

> Away with that audacious lady! Antigonus,
> I charged thee that she should not come about me.
> I knew she would.   *(Act 2 Scene 3, lines 42–4)*

Shakespeare makes it clear that Leontes has relied on Paulina for 16 years: 'My true Paulina, / We shall not marry till thou bid'st us' (Act 5 Scene 1, lines 81–2) and 'O grave and good Paulina, the great comfort / That I have had of thee!' (Act 5 Scene 3, lines 1–2). The audience is told during Act 5 Scene 2 that the statue 'is in the keeping of Paulina', and that she has 'privately twice or thrice a day ever since the death of Hermione visited that removed house'.

Shakespeare acknowledges that the position of women at the time was that they were nominally and legally subject to their husbands. In practice there were many individual women like Paulina who did not fit into the conventional mould.

Childbirth

Having children was a risky business for women in Jacobean times. It was even less safe for the babies. One of the reasons why the 'average' life span of Jacobeans is often spoken of as being relatively short, is because of the number of children who died within their first five years. Emilia speaks of Hermione's baby as being 'Lusty' (healthy) and 'like to live'. Unusually for high-status women of the time, it seems that Hermione is forced by circumstances to breast-feed the baby in prison. At her trial she speaks of the baby:

> My third comfort,
> Starred most unluckily, is from my breast –
> The innocent milk in it most innocent mouth –
> Haled out to murder.   *(Act 3 Scene 2, lines 96–9)*

But Leontes has earlier spoken of the fact that she did not feed Mamillius herself: 'I am glad you did not nurse him'. Tradition allowed women a time indoors after giving birth; fresh air was considered unhealthy for invalids. Hermione has been rushed to the open court before she has regained her 'strength of limit'.

Male friendships

There was a strongly expressed feeling in Shakespeare's time, both in conversation and in the literature of the time, that the friendship of men was in some way superior to any relationship with women. Women were held to be creatures of passion who evoked undesirable emotions in men, such as the extreme jealousy experienced by Leontes. Shakespeare gives the friendship between Leontes and Polixenes great emphasis: 'there rooted betwixt them then such an affection which cannot choose but branch now'. There has apparently been regular contact between them through, 'gifts, letters, loving embassies'.

Polixenes draws attention to the potential corruption of association with women when he compares his boyhood friendship with Leontes to that of 'twinned lambs that did frisk i'th'sun' and to the fact that their relationship was entirely innocent, 'we knew not / The doctrine of ill-doing, nor dreamed / That any did'. He refers to his wife and to Hermione as 'Temptations'. Though her tone is light-hearted, Hermione warns him not to take this line of argument to its conclusion in case he suggests that 'Your queen and I are devils'. She too refers to sex, even within a faithful marriage, as 'offences'. It seems significant that at the play's end, together with his happiness at being reunited with his wife and daughter whom he had long thought dead, Leontes seems overjoyed to welcome Polixenes (Act 5 Scene 2, lines 35–7), and refers to him in the play's final speech as 'my brother'.

Religion, grace and redemption

Mentioning God, even obliquely, had been banned on the English stage by the time Shakespeare wrote *The Winter's Tale*. As part of the Act for the Uniformity of Common Prayer in 1559 there was a general and unspecific ban on any 'derogation, depraving or despising of the Book of Common Prayer', and this had been interpreted stringently by Edmund Tilney when he became the Master of the Revels in 1581. The Master of the Revels had to approve any play before it could be performed. The law was made even more restrictive by King James in 1606. Shakespeare avoided potential trouble by giving *The Winter's Tale* a pagan setting, but evidence of contemporary religious beliefs and practices are evident in the play.

Although some critics have been attacked for over-imposing a specifically Christian interpretation on *The Winter's Tale* (see page

90), it would be equally foolish to deny that there are many references to Christian theology. The references to the innocence of childhood made by Polixenes (Act 1 Scene 2, lines 67–75) are frequently interpreted as a reference to the doctrine of Original Sin: the idea that mankind is innately sinful and can only be redeemed by the grace of God. Throughout the play both Hermione and Perdita are associated with the word 'grace', which can mean a kind of nobility of behaviour, but was much more commonly used in Shakespeare's time to mean the favour of God which leads to salvation. In contemporary belief, grace could not be earned or deserved, but it could be forfeited. The structure of *The Winter's Tale* reflects the Christian concept that there must be true contrition for any wrongdoing before there can be forgiveness. Leontes spends 16 years in repentance for his sins, and Cleomenes speaks of his 'saint-like sorrow' (Act 5 Scene 1, lines 1–2). However, Shakespeare deliberately moves away from a specifically Christian conclusion: the restoration of Hermione is not conditional upon his repentance, but on the fulfilment of the oracle and the discovery of Perdita.

Act 3 Scene 1, where Cleomenes and Dion describe their visit to the Temple of Apollo at Delphos, is full of references to the sacredness of the temple and the spiritual effect the experience has had on them. Their expressions of religious faith contrast with the horror of Leontes' suspicions. Although the references are to Apollo's temple, the tone of the scene is one of religious reverence, which would have been instantly apparent and appealing to a Jacobean Christian audience. The final line of the scene is 'And gracious be the issue!' The rejection of Apollo's oracle in Scene 2 is likely to have been experienced by a contemporary audience with a corresponding sense of outrage and sacrilege.

Shakespeare's alertness to troublesome aspects of contemporary religious belief is made evident in the final scene, when Paulina makes it clear that Hermione's statue is in a chapel and that she is guarding herself against the accusation of witchcraft:

> But then you'll think –
> Which I protest against – I am assisted
> By wicked powers.   *(Act 5 Scene 3, lines 89–91)*

In Elizabethan and Jacobean England there was a strong belief in the existence of witches and a fear of witchcraft. James I was particularly interested in witchcraft and had written a book on demonology. Shakespeare had already exploited this interest in *Macbeth*. In the statue scene in *The Winter's Tale* he is particularly careful to avoid any accusation that he is resurrecting Hermione from the dead by witchcraft, and Paulina asks those present to 'awake [their] faith' before commanding the music to awake Hermione.

Some critics argue that Shakespeare was a secret Catholic, and the Christian interpretation of *The Winter's Tale* is frequently used to support this claim. However, it is possible to interpret 'grace' as a secular quality of nobility and to interpret the play as an exploration of seasonal renewal. Arguing against an over-emphasised stress on the Christian interpretation of the play, the critic Derek Traversi says:

> It seems to me to be no more than natural that a writer of his time and place should be aware of Christian tradition as an influence moulding his thought and that he should even seek, in his latest plays, to present in terms of a highly personal reading of that tradition some of his final conclusions about life.

Theatre

For some Elizabethans and Jacobeans the theatre was an important arena for the display and discussion of current intellectual and political debate. But the authorities viewed the theatre with suspicion. Not only were plays censored for their possible seditious or anti-authority content, but also the times when theatres could open were strictly controlled. For example, they could not show plays during times of plague or on Sundays, and plays had to finish in time for the audience to be home before sunset. In 1596, the City of London authorities banned public performances of plays within the square mile of the city. Puritans, too, thought that theatre led to freedom of discussion in matters best left to authority. For Puritans, theatre was an invitation to licentiousness with its cross-dressing and portrayal of love and sex. But the theatre had its defenders. Shakespeare gave Hamlet lines that expressed an incisively powerful justification of its role and purpose in society: 'to hold as 'twere the mirror up to nature; to show virtue her own feature, scorn her own image, and the very age and body of the time his form and pressure'. And Thomas Nashe wrote a powerful defence of the theatre in the 1590s, responding to the attacks made on the theatre by the Puritans:

> In plays, all cozenages, all cunning drifts over-gilded
> with outward holiness, all stratagems of war, all the
> cankerworms that breed on the rust of peace, are most lively
> anatomized; they show the ill success of treason, the fall of
> hasty climbers, the wretched end of usurpers, the misery of
> civil dissension, and how just God is evermore in punishing
> of murther.

Many of Shakespeare's plays make explicit references to the idea of the theatre and acting being an image of life. In *Macbeth* the image is disturbing. Man becomes a 'poor player / That struts and frets his hour upon the stage / And then is heard no more.' Even in the well-known Seven Ages of Man speech in *As You Like It*, men and women are 'merely players'. The comparison of a person's life to an actor's brief part also occurs in the work of Shakespeare's contemporaries, suggesting that it was a widespread view at the time.

One of the main themes of *The Winter's Tale* is the idea of playing a part. Linguistically, the theme of playing links Leontes and Perdita. He harps on the idea of 'playing':

> Go play, boy, play: thy mother plays, and I
> Play too – but so disgraced a part whose issue
> Will hiss me to my grave.   *(Act 1 Scene 2, lines 187–9)*

Perdita also refers to the fact that she is playing a part by her references to her costume: 'Most goddess-like pranked up', 'in these my borrowed flaunts'. She makes an even more specific reference to playing a role when she says:

> Methinks I play as I have seen them do
> In Whitsun pastorals; sure this robe of mine
> Does change my disposition.   *(Act 4 Scene 4, lines 133–5)*

Both Camillo and Paulina direct parts of the plot, giving the characters their roles and actions. Camillo instructs Polixenes in the precise manner of his escape from Sicilia and in Act 4 Scene 4 organises the escape of Perdita and Florizel with an explicit reference to the theatre, 'as if / The scene you play were mine', and Perdita concedes, 'I see the play so lies / That I must bear a part.' Another feature that testifies to Shakespeare's reputation as an actors' playwright is that in few other plays are there quite so many implicit stage directions about the position and behaviour of the characters.

Time

A sense of the cycles of life and death and of the seasons was particularly pertinent to Jacobean thought. Arising particularly from Renaissance thinking, the dualities of winter and spring, youth and age, court and country, art and nature, joy and sorrow, were central to cultural and intellectual considerations. Shakespeare uses the theme of time to explore all these issues.

The story of *The Winter's Tale* is structured around the seasons of the year as experienced through Jacobean cultural and religious traditions. It begins in winter, traditionally a time of hospitality. Lent is the season of repentance and Whitsun the time of the summer festival. Autumn is the time of harvest, and at the end of the play Leontes looks forward to the renewal of the cycle when he greets Florizel and Perdita, 'Welcome hither, / As is the spring to th'earth!'

Time is an important theme in *The Winter's Tale*, as it is in Shakespeare's *Sonnets*. The effects of the action of time is a theme of much Renaissance literature, with time frequently being portrayed as the stealer of youth and beauty, or as a destroyer. Shakespeare goes beyond the conventional image and has his figure of Time explicitly speak of being one that 'makes and unfolds error'.

From the opening of the play, where Archidamus and Camillo are looking back to the childhood friendship of Leontes and Polixenes and forward to the visit which will be paid 'this coming summer', the audience is made aware of the passage of time. Polixenes speaks very precisely of the length of his visit, 'Nine changes of the wat'ry star', and during the exchanges in Act 1 there is a sense of speed as Leontes moves rapidly from suspicion to certainty. This culminates in the haste with which Polixenes and Camillo leave Sicilia: 'Please your highness / To take the urgent hour. Come, sir, away!'

Act 2 begins immediately their escape is discovered, as the audience witnesses Leontes receiving news of the flight of Camillo and Polixenes. Leontes has already sent Cleomenes and Dion to

Apollo's temple, and there is great emphasis on the speed of their journey. The baby is only recently born when Paulina takes her to Leontes, who orders Antigonus to abandon her. He takes the baby off immediately. During the trial scene, the deaths of Mamillius and Hermione follow each other rapidly and it is not until the gentle rhythm of Time's speech that the audience has time to catch breath.

By contrast, Act 4 Scene 4, the longest scene in the play, seems to invoke the long days of summer. The festival is celebrating a very successful sheep-shearing and emphasises the importance of the farming community to the Jacobean economy. It reminds the audience that although time passes there are also the cycles of birth, growth and death, and the changing seasons. Perdita's description of seasonal change is unusual and draws attention to the interdependence of the seasons:

> Sir, the year growing ancient,
> Not yet on summer's death nor on the birth
> Of trembling winter   *(Act 4 Scene 4, lines 79–81)*

In Act 5, with the return to Sicilia there is also something of a return to the speed of action of the early part of the play, particularly in Scene 3 with the relation by the Gentlemen of the discovery of Perdita's parentage and the death of Antigonus. During the statue scene there is a moment of stillness as the audience on and off stage views Hermione and is reminded of the passage of 'the wide gap of time' by Hermione's wrinkles. However, there is a return to the sense of the quick passage of time, as the play ends on a slightly surprising rush: 'Hastily lead away.'

Language

In Edward Bond's play *Bingo*, a fictional dramatisation of Shakespeare's final years in Stratford-upon-Avon, Shakespeare meets Ben Jonson for a drinking session. As they get more and more drunk together, Jonson remarks, 'Your recent stuff's been pretty peculiar. What was *The Winter's Tale* about?'

As the section on Critical approaches shows (pages 86–107), Jonson is only the first of many who have expressed their bafflement about *The Winter's Tale*. Some of that puzzlement arises because of the play's language, which has been called an example of 'Shakespeare's late style' or, far less flatteringly, 'clotted', 'congested', 'disjointed', 'tormented with allusion', 'knotty', 'obscure' and other uncomplimentary descriptions.

Certainly most critics have agreed that the language of the play presents difficulties. But many of the problems of tortuous syntax, obscure vocabulary and elusive rhythms arise from, and are particularly expressive of, the subject matter of the play, notably Leontes' disturbed mental state. The complexities of the language catch the nature of his disordered thoughts and feelings with uncanny precision. From the beginning of the twentieth century, with modernism's liking for verbal difficulty, and with psychoanalysis' interest in the language of troubled minds, the language of the play became regarded increasingly favourably. It should also be noted that the language is not uniformly difficult. At times it is simple and transparently clear in its expression of deep emotion: 'O, she's warm!'

Ben Jonson famously remarked that Shakespeare 'wanted art' (lacked technical skill). But Jonson's comment is mistaken, as is the popular image of Shakespeare as a 'natural' writer, utterly spontaneous, inspired only by his imagination. Shakespeare possessed a profound knowledge of the language techniques of his own and previous times. Behind the apparent effortlessness of the language lies a deeply practised skill. That skill is evident in *The Winter's Tale* in all kinds of ways. The play displays a wide variety of language registers. The pervasive wordplay reflects the way that Shakespeare plays with language to explore multi-level meanings. It constantly reminds the audience of the duplicity of language.

By the time he came to write *The Winter's Tale*, Shakespeare had written at least 34 plays. He was a restless experimenter, and in his 'late plays' (the four 'romances', see page 53) he had left far behind the style of his early plays with their regular rhythms, carefully developed images, end-stopped lines and speeches characterised by logical connections and development. Now much of his language becomes compressed, seemingly awkward and jarring, with violent conjunctions of images and thought, but with its 'otherness' particularly suitable to the archaic, fairy-tale quality of his drama.

But for all such distinctive (and sometimes daunting) qualities of the language of *The Winter's Tale*, Shakespeare employs in the play the same language techniques he had used throughout his entire playwriting career in order to intensify dramatic effect, create mood and character, and so produce memorable theatre. Those techniques are found alike in the play's prose and verse. What follows are some of those language techniques. As you read them, always keep in mind that Shakespeare wrote for the stage, and that actors will therefore employ a wide variety of both verbal and non-verbal methods to exploit the dramatic possibilities of the language. They will use the full range of their voices and accompany the words with appropriate expressions, gestures and actions.

Imagery

The Winter's Tale abounds in imagery (sometimes called 'figures' or 'figurative language'): vivid words and phrases that help create the atmosphere of the play as they conjure up emotionally charged mental pictures in the imagination. Shakespeare seems to have thought in images, and the whole play richly demonstrates his unflagging and varied use of verbal illustration, particularly in his use of natural images. When Leontes says to Mamillius, 'Look on me with your welkin eye', he is suggesting far more than just the idea of Mamillius having sky-blue eyes. He is evoking the innocence of the heavens and also referring back to the idea of Mamillius being a child who 'physics the subject'.

Early critics such as Doctor Johnson and John Dryden were critical of Shakespeare's fondness for imagery. They felt that many images obscured meaning and detracted attention from the subjects they represented. Over the past 200 years, however, critics, poets and audiences have increasingly valued Shakespeare's imagery. They recognise how he uses it to give pleasure as it stirs the audience's imagination, deepens the dramatic impact of particular moments or moods, provides insight into character, and intensifies meaning and emotional force. Images carry powerful significance far deeper than their surface meanings, and some critics have detected dominant or repeated images ('iterative imagery') running through the play, as for example Caroline Spurgeon's identification of the 'common flow of life through all things' (see page 94).

As the section on Contexts shows, Shakespeare's Jacobean world provides much of the play's imagery. In Act 1, Hermione speaks of 'thwacking' Polixenes 'hence with distaffs' (the stick onto which wool was spun, and a symbol of female domesticity), and of loving Leontes, 'not a jar o'th'clock behind / What lady she her lord'. Leontes thinks that Hermione is 'Still virginalling / Upon his palm' (fingering his hand as though it were the keyboard of a virginal).

Shakespeare's imagery uses metaphor, simile or personification. All are comparisons which in effect substitute one thing (the image) for another (the thing described).

A **simile** compares one thing to another using 'like' or 'as'. Leontes says that he and Mamillius are 'as like as eggs'. When Leontes speaks of Polixenes as someone who 'wears' Hermione 'like her medal, hanging / About his neck', the picture evoked is both of possession and of physical contact, and it is echoed in Act 5 Scene 3 by Camillo: 'She hangs about his neck.' Polixenes asks Camillo to 'Make me not sighted like the basilisk', a mythical monster which could kill with just a look.

Florizel and Perdita play with similes in Act 4 when she says she wishes to 'strew' him with flowers. He asks 'like a corse?' (dead body). She rejects his image by choosing another: 'No, like a bank for love to lie and play on'. Then she returns to his image of a supine body with the mildly sexual image of 'not to be buried, / But quick and in mine arms' ('quick' has the double meaning of alive, and sexually aroused). Florizel says that Perdita's hand is 'soft as dove's down'. On at least five occasions, accounts of what has happened in the play are spoken of as being 'like an old tale'.

A **metaphor** is also a comparison, suggesting that two dissimilar things are actually the same. Leontes speaks of the dagger he wore as a child as if it were a dog with a muzzle over its mouth: 'my dagger muzzled, / Lest it should bite its master'. The metaphors used by

Leontes in Act 1 Scene 2 (lines 185–207) graphically reflect the sexual disgust he is feeling: 'she has been sluiced in's absence, / And his pond fished by his next neighbour'. He compares her to property: 'Whiles other men have gates, and those gates opened, / As mine, against their will', and to a besieged city:

> No barricado for a belly. Know't,
> It will let in and out the enemy
> With bag and baggage. *(Act 1 Scene 2, lines 204–6)*

Shakespeare symbolises the tortured state of Leontes' mind with powerful imagery. Leontes uses the image of bed-sheets to represent the chastity of his marriage defiled by Hermione's imagined adultery, 'Sully the purity and whiteness of my sheets – / Which to preserve is sleep'. His mind is described as suffering physical pain, attacked by 'goads, thorns, nettles, tails of wasps'. When he is trying to explain how he feels to his courtiers he uses the image of the spider which only causes revulsion when perceived: 'I have drunk, and seen the spider'. (A common belief of the time was that spiders were only poisonous if seen.)

When the shepherd describes Florizel's manner towards Perdita he evokes a very precise picture, associating the lovers with the natural elements of moon and water:

> for never gazed the moon
> Upon the water as he'll stand and read,
> As 'twere, my daughter's eyes *(Act 4 Scene 4, lines 172–4)*

To put it another way, a metaphor borrows one word or phrase to express another, as for example when Camillo describes Florizel to Autolycus as being 'half flayed already', he is using a metaphor which compares the removing of clothes to skinning someone.

Personification turns all kinds of things into persons, giving them human feelings or attributes. Time is the most obvious example of personification in the play. Florizel uses an extreme image to suggest his despair when his father and Camillo arrive in Sicilia and it seems that he will never marry Perdita: 'The stars, I see, will kiss the valleys first'. Elsewhere Perdita speaks of the sun as though it could take deliberate action:

The self-same sun that shines upon his court
Hides not his visage from our cottage but
Looks on alike.   *(Act 4 Scene 4, lines 423–5)*

Classical mythology contributes to the richness of the play's imagery. Elizabethans were usually more familiar with such references than are most members of audiences today. Jacobean audiences would recognise Florizel's reference to Perdita's being 'no shepherdess, but Flora / Peering in April's front' (Flora was the goddess of Spring) and would know the stories which told of the 'transformations' the gods took for love:

> Jupiter
> Became a bull, and bellowed; the green Neptune
> A ram, and bleated; and the fire-robed god,
> Golden Apollo, a poor humble swain,
> As I seem now.   *(Act 4 Scene 4, lines 27–31)*

Shakespeare's contemporary audience would also have known that in these stories the gods transformed themselves to fulfil their desires, which is why Florizel has to disclaim any sexual intentions: 'my desires / Run not before mine honour, nor my lusts / Burn hotter than my faith'. When Perdita regrets that she has no flowers of spring to give to the shepherdesses and Florizel, she refers to the myth of Proserpina, who was abducted by Dis, god of the Underworld, 'O Proserpina, / For the flowers now that, frighted, thou let'st fall / From Dis's waggon!', and she describes the violets as 'sweeter than the lids of Juno's eyes / Or Cytherea's breath'.

Antithesis

Antithesis is the opposition of words or phrases against each other, as in 'Thou met'st with things dying, I with things new born', and in Perdita's words to the 'statue' of her mother, 'Dear queen, that ended when I but began', each opposing death with birth. This setting of word against word is one of Shakespeare's favourite language devices and he uses it extensively in all his plays. Why? Because antithesis powerfully expresses conflict through its use of opposites, and conflict is the essence of all drama. In *The Winter's Tale*, this conflict occurs in many forms: tragedy against comedy, Sicilia against Bohemia, court against country, loss against recovery, birth against death. It is particularly associated with the seasons. Polixenes says that his son 'makes a July's day short as December', Autolycus sings, 'the red blood reigns in the winter's pale', and Perdita describes autumn as 'Not yet on summer's death nor on the birth / Of trembling winter'.

Antithesis intensifies the sense of conflict, and embodies its different forms. Polixenes compares the innocence of childhood with the corruption of maturity when he claims that if 'our weak spirits ne'er been higher reared / With stronger blood', he and Leontes would have remained free from sin. Leontes instructs Hermione ironically to 'Let what is dear in Sicily be cheap'. Hermione speaks of her inability to weep: 'I have / That honourable grief lodged here which burns / Worse than tears drown'. When Leontes discovers his errors, he uses antithesis to compare himself to Camillo:

> How he glisters
> Thorough my rust! And how his piety
> Does my deeds make the blacker!   (Act 3 Scene 2, lines 167–9)

Repetition

Different forms of language repetition run through the play, contributing to its atmosphere, creation of character, and dramatic impact, especially perhaps in the rising hysteria in Leontes' repeated 'nothing' on which, ironically, he has built all his suspicions. There is a pun here on 'nothing' and 'noting'. 'Noting' means knowing, which also has the connotation of carnal knowledge:

> Is this nothing?
> Why then the world and all that's in't is nothing,
> The covering sky is nothing, Bohemia nothing,
> My wife is nothing, nor nothing have these nothings,
> If this be nothing.   (Act 1 Scene 2, lines 292–6)

In the first part of *The Winter's Tale* Shakespeare uses repetition in a very specific way to suggest the unreliability of language to Leontes' diseased mind. Again and again, Leontes picks up a word used either by himself or by someone else and repeats it with a different meaning: when Leontes says Mamillius must be 'neat', his mind moves from tidy to horned cattle; he uses various meanings of the word 'play'.

Camillo innocently says that Polixenes stays to 'satisfy' Hermione's 'entreaties' and Leontes immediately interprets 'satisfy' in its sexual sense. Hermione is a frequent victim of his capacity to read another meaning into a word, as with 'sport' (Act 2 Scene 1, lines 58–61), 'mistake' (Act 2 Scene 1, lines 81–2, 100), and 'dreams' (Act 3 Scene 2, lines 79–80).

Shakespeare's skill in using repetition to heighten theatrical effect and deepen emotional and imaginative significance is most evident in particular speeches. Repeated words, phrases, rhythms and sounds add intensity to the moment or episode, perhaps most famously in Florizel's loving praise of Perdita in Act 4 Scene 4 (lines 135–46).

Repetition is used to similar effect in the play's prose as well as its verse; as, for example, in the message from Apollo's oracle (Act 3 Scene 2, lines 130–3), and in Autolycus' speech when he is pretending to be a courtier (Act 4 Scene 4, lines 689–96). Shakespeare also uses repetition to emphasise the ridiculous claim by the Clown that he is 'a gentleman born'. In verse, Shakespeare uses repeated patterns of phrasing and rhythm, for example, for rhetorical effect in Hermione's speech at her trial in Act 3 Scene 2, particularly in lines 35–43 and 94–104. These repeated patterns of phrasing and rhythm also occur in Polixenes' description of Leontes' jealousy:

> as she's rare
> Must it be great; and as his person's mighty
> Must it be violent; and as he does conceive
> He is dishonoured by a man which ever
> Professed to him, why, his revenges must
> In that be made more bitter. (Act 1 Scene 2, lines 452–7)

Repetition also occasionally occurs in rhyme; in *The Winter's Tale* there are few rhyming couplets except for Time's speech with its 16 pairs of couplets to represent the 16 years. Here Shakespeare is using a consciously old-fashioned technique, which he parodies when he makes Autolycus complete a couplet unconsciously begun by the Shepherd:

SHEPHERD   None, sir; I have no pheasant, cock nor hen.
AUTOLYCUS   How blest are we that are not simple men!
> (Act 4 Scene 4, lines 702–3)

Lists

One of Shakespeare's favourite techniques is to accumulate words or phrases rather like a list. He had learned the technique as a schoolboy in Stratford-upon-Avon, and his skill in knowing how to use lists dramatically is evident in the many examples in *The Winter's Tale*. He intensifies and varies description, atmosphere and argument as he 'piles up' item on item, incident on incident. Sometimes the list comprises only single words or phrases, 'goads, thorns, nettles, tails of wasps' (Act 1 Scene 2, line 329) or 'Nor brass, nor stone, nor parchment' (Act 1 Scene 2, line 360). Some lists are brief descriptions, ('As o'er-dyed blacks, as wind, as waters, false / As dice'). Other lists are more extended, as for example the servant's list of the contents of the pedlar's pack which serves to enhance Autolycus' own description of it in his song. Yet others are lengthy character portrayals, such as Autolycus' description of himself:

> He hath been since an ape-bearer; then a process-server, a
> bailiff; then he compassed a motion of the Prodigal Son, and
> married a tinker's wife within a mile where my land and living
> lies; and having flown over many knavish professions, he
> settled only in rogue.   *(Act 4 Scene 3, lines 81–5)*

Such 'character lists' are found in different forms. Perdita's list of flowers that she would like to be able to give the shepherdesses and Florizel serves also to strengthen the audience's impression of her learning and innate culture (Act 4 Scene 4, lines 118–27). Other lists give a very evocative picture of the state of the character's mind. This is particularly true of Leontes' list of the imagined actions of Hermione and Polixenes in Act 1 Scene 2, lines 284–292. Florizel's list of the things he would sacrifice before he would break his oath to Perdita testifies to the exuberance of his love:

> Not for Bohemia, nor the pomp that may
> Be thereat gleaned, for all the sun sees, or
> The close earth wombs, or the profound seas hides
> In unknown fathoms, will I break my oath
>
> *(Act 4 Scene 4, lines 467–70)*

Paulina has some particularly effective lists: her description of the baby's likeness to Leontes (Act 2 Scene 3, lines 99–102) serves to lighten the bleakness of the scene a little, and also to remind the audience of Leontes' own concern about Mamillius' resemblance to him. The punishments she demands from Leontes (Act 3 Scene 2, lines 172–4) draw attention to the horror of the effects of Leontes' jealous frenzy: and her list of instructions to the statue of Hermione (Act 5 Scene 3, lines 99–103) demonstrate her role as director of the last part of the fulfilment of the oracle.

The many lists in the play provide valuable opportunities for actors to vary their delivery. In speaking, a character usually seeks to give each 'item' a distinctiveness in emphasis and emotional tone, and sometimes an accompanying action and expression. In addition, the accumulating effect of lists can add to the force of argument, enrich atmosphere, amplify meaning and provide extra dimensions of character.

Verse and prose

About two-thirds of the play is in verse, one-third is in prose. How did Shakespeare decide whether to write in verse or prose? One answer is that he followed theatrical convention. Prose was often used by comic and low-status characters. High-status characters spoke verse. 'Comic' scenes were written in prose but audiences expected verse in 'serious' scenes: the poetic style was thought to be particularly suitable for lovers and for moments of high dramatic or emotional intensity.

Shakespeare used his judgement about which convention or principle he should follow in *The Winter's Tale*, and it is obvious that he frequently broke the 'rules'. Perdita and Florizel as lovers speak in verse, but in many episodes so does the Shepherd, even though he is both comic and low status.

The verse of *The Winter's Tale* is varied, but it is mainly in blank verse: unrhymed verse written in iambic pentameter. It is conventional to define iambic pentameter as a metre in which each line has five stressed syllables (/) alternating with five unstressed syllables (×):

> × / × / × / × / × /
> The bug which you would fright me with, I seek.

At school, Shakespeare had learned the technical definition of iambic pentameter. In Greek 'penta' means five, and 'iamb' means a 'foot' of two syllables, the first unstressed, the second stressed, as in 'alas' = aLAS. Shakespeare practised writing in that metre, and his early plays, such as *Titus Andronicus* or *Richard III*, are very regular in rhythm (often expressed as de-DUM de-DUM de-DUM de-DUM de-DUM) and with each line 'end-stopped' (making sense on its own).

By the time he came to write *The Winter's Tale* (around 1611), Shakespeare had become very flexible and experimental in his use of iambic pentameter. The 'five-beat' metre is still present but the 'natural' rhythm of speech is played off against it. End-stopped lines are less frequent. There is greater use of *enjambement* (running on) where one line flows on into the next, seemingly with little or no pause, as in Leontes' words:

> I chose
> Camillo for the minister to poison
> My friend Polixenes; which had been done,
> But that the good mind of Camillo tardied
> My swift command, though I with death and with
> Reward did threaten and encourage him,
> Not doing it and being done.   *(Act 3 Scene 2, lines 156–62)*

Shakespeare's flexibility in his use of the form of blank verse enables him to reflect accurately the mood and intention of the character, matching form and content. Examples include the soft sounds and elisions of Hermione's demands (Act 1 Scene 2, lines 90–101) and the complex and disturbed thoughts of Leontes:

> Affection, thy intention stabs the centre.
> Thou dost make possible things not so held,
> Communicat'st with dreams – how can this be? –
> With what's unreal thou coactive art,
> And fellow'st nothing. Then 'tis very credent
> Thou mayst co-join with something; and thou dost,
> And that beyond commission, and I find it,
> And that to the infection of my brains
> And hard'ning of my brows.   *(Act 1 Scene 2, lines 138–46)*

Some critics, directors and actors have strong convictions about how the verse should be spoken. For example, the director Peter Hall insists there should always be a pause at the end of each line. But it seems appropriate when studying (or watching or acting in) *The Winter's Tale*, not to attempt to apply rigid rules about verse-speaking. Shakespeare certainly used the convention of iambic pentameter, but he did not adhere to it slavishly. He knew 'the rules', but he was not afraid to break them to suit his dramatic purposes. No one knows for sure just how the lines were delivered on Shakespeare's own stage, and today actors use their discretion in how to deliver the lines. They pause or emphasise to convey meaning and emotion and to avoid the mechanical or clockwork-sounding speech that a too slavish attention to the pentameter line might produce.

In *The Winter's Tale*, many of the lines are shared between two characters, possibly more than in any other play. This ensures that, though the characters are speaking in verse, the cadence of the lines is closer to that of ordinary speech. Convention suggests that this sharing of a line of verse implies that there is little break between one character speaking and the next in order to maintain the rhythm of the line. Actors today are usually very flexible in their approach to the question of shared lines.

Critical approaches

The poet and critic W H Auden once wrote that critics should be forced to declare their tastes so that anyone reading the criticism would be able to understand the point of view of the critic. Critics have viewed *The Winter's Tale* in widely differing ways and their own tastes and predilections necessarily inform their points of view. The following section gives you some idea of the divergent critical views of *The Winter's Tale*.

Traditional criticism

Early commentators on *The Winter's Tale* often held the play in low esteem. Dryden, writing in 1672, lumped it together with *Love's Labour's Lost* and *Measure for Measure* and said they were all 'either grounded on impossibilities, or at least so meanly written that the comedy neither caused your mirth, nor the serious part your concernment'. Alexander Pope thought that Shakespeare had only written part of the play, and in 1753 Charlotte Lennox wrote in *Shakespeare Illustrated* that she considered parts of it 'absurd and ridiculous'. Lennox objected to the characterisation of Hermione and particularly to the statue scene. She questioned:

> how can it be imagined that Hermione, a virtuous and
> affectionate wife, would conceal herself during sixteen years in
> a solitary house . . . ? How ridiculous also in a great Queen, on
> so interesting an occasion, to submit to such buffoonery as
> standing on a pedestal, motionless, her eyes fixed, and at last
> to be conjured down by a magical command of Paulina.

Samuel Johnson, the major eighteenth-century scholar and critic, also seemed unenthusiastic about the play. In particular he thought that the narrative by the Gentlemen in Act 5 Scene 2 was Shakespeare's way of saving himself time and work. Johnson would have preferred a dramatisation of the meeting of the two kings, and for the audience to witness Leontes' recognition of Perdita (a view that is discussed on page 89). By the early nineteenth century, with the growth of Romanticism, critics judged the play more positively. However, they tended to focus either on character or on moral lessons to be learned from the play. Some also assumed that analysis of the play could make Shakespeare himself known and understood as a person.

William Hazlitt, in 1817, was impressed by the pastoral elements of the play. He agreed with those like Pope who criticised the structure and anachronisms of the play, but defended the play in spite of them:

> These slips or blemishes however do not prove it not to be Shakespeare's; for he was as like to fall into them as anybody; but we do not know anybody but himself who could produce the beauties.

Hazlitt valued stage performances of *The Winter's Tale*, and considered it 'one of the best-acting of our author's plays'. But Hazlitt's style is typical of a great deal of traditional character criticism. One aspect calls for immediate comment: his use of the first person plural ('we', 'us', 'our'), as in his comment 'we still read the courtship of Florizel and Perdita, as we welcome the return of spring, with the same feelings as ever'. It is a style that has bedevilled critical writing right up to the present time. Like all critics who use 'we', Hazlitt was reporting his own personal response to the play, but attempting to pass it off as something everybody feels (or should feel). Such use of language is suspect, because many people simply do not share the sympathies expressed. As noted in the Organising your responses section of this Guide, the use of 'we', 'our', etc. is best avoided in your own writing.

Writing in 1822, Mrs Inchbald belongs to the same school of criticism as Charlotte Lennox. Having decided upon her interpretation of how particular characters might act in the real world, she imposes her own moral opinions about how the characters should behave in the play:

> There are two occurrences in the drama, quite as improbable as the unprovoked jealousy of Leontes, – the one, that the gentle, the amiable, the tender Perdita should be an unconcerned spectator of the doom which menaced her foster, and supposed real, father; and carelessly forsake him in the midst of his calamities. The other disgraceful improbability is, – that the young prince Florizel should introduce himself to the Court of Sicilia, by speaking arrant falsehoods.

The critical style of writing about characters as if they were real people continued throughout the nineteenth century. In 1851, Hartley Coleridge concentrated very much on character analysis, and displayed the judgemental approach and florid style of the time:

> Except Autolycus, none of the characters show much of Shakespeare's philosophic depth . . . Hermione is frank and noble, rising in dignity as she falls in fortune . . . in sunshine a butterfly, in misery a martyr. Paulina is an honest scold. Perdita a pretty piece of poetry. Polixenes is not very amiable, nor, in truth, much of anything. The length of time he remains witness to his son's courtship, before he discovers himself, is a sacrifice to effect. Camillo is an old rogue whom I can hardly forgive for his double treachery. The Shepherd and his son are well enough in their way; but Mopsa and Dorcas might be countrified enough with better tongues in their heads. Of the rest nothing need be said.

Similar judgements of characters led some critics to identify what they saw as the moral teachings of *The Winter's Tale*. F J Furnivall confidently claimed in 1877:

> Its purpose, its lesson, are to teach forgiveness of wrongs, not vengeance for them; to give the sinner time to repent and amend, not to cut him off in his sin; to frustrate the crimes he has purposed.

The predilection for finding Shakespeare's own biography in the plays is evident in Edward Dowden's *Shakspere – His Mind and Art*, 1875. Dowden related his interpretation of *The Winter's Tale* to his knowledge of Shakespeare's life, almost as though he were personally acquainted with Shakespeare's actions and emotions:

> Serenity Shakspere did attain. Once again before the end, his mirth is bright and tender. When in some Warwickshire field, one breezy morning, as the daffodil began to peer, the poet conceived his Autolycus, there might seem to be almost a return of the lightheartedness of youth. But the same play that contains Autolycus contains the grave and noble figure of

Hermione. From its elevation and calm Shakspere's heart can pass into the simple merriment of rustic festivity; he can enjoy the open-mouthed happiness of country clowns; he is delighted by the gay defiance of order and honesty which Autolycus, most charming of rogues, professes; he is touched and exquisitely thrilled by the pure and vivid joy of Perdita among her flowers. Now that Shakspere is most a householder he enters most into the pleasures of truantship.

Responding to Dowden's style of analysis of *The Winter's Tale*, Lytton Strachey, a great debunker of nineteenth-century values and persons, wrote in 1906 that it is a 'pretty picture, but is it true? . . . Modern critics, in their eagerness to appraise everything that is beautiful and good at its proper value, seem to have entirely forgotten that there is another side to the medal.' Strachey goes on to identify in the late plays 'portraits of peculiar infamy', 'wickedness', 'figures of discord and evil'. He draws a quite different conclusion from that of the gushing judgements of many earlier critics: 'Nowhere, indeed, is Shakespeare's violence of expression more constantly displayed than in the "gentle utterances" of his last period.'

Many critics have in particular objected to what they feel are faults in the construction of *The Winter's Tale*. Sir Arthur Quiller-Couch, writing in 1915, echoes Doctor Johnson's criticism (see above): 'This brings us to the greatest fault of all; to the recognition scene; or rather to the scamping of it'. A quarter of a century later, Mark Van Doren agreed with Quiller-Couch:

Shakespeare disappoints our expectation in one important respect. The recognition of Leontes and his daughter takes place off stage: we only hear three gentlemen talking prose about it (Vii), and are denied the satisfaction of such a scene as we might have supposed would crown the play. The reason may be that Shakespeare was weary of a plot which already had complicated itself beyond comfort; or that a recognition scene appeared in his mind more due to Hermione, considering the age and degree of her sufferings, than to that 'most peerless piece of earth' Perdita. In poetic justice he gave it to Hermione, and we have the business of a statue coming to life while music plays. But the poetry he actually had written required that Perdita should have it. Perhaps he could not imagine – though this itself is hard to imagine – what Leontes would say. For Leontes had done what no words, even Shakespeare's words, could utterly undo. Mamillius and Antigonus had lost their lives, an oracle had been blasphemed, a wife had been slandered, love had been defiled.

As the twentieth century progressed, critical opinion continued to find much to fault as well as to praise in the play. In 1947, S L Bethell made an impassioned defence of *The Winter's Tale* in language that almost seems more like censure. Although he admired the subject matter and thought that the play was a Christian allegory, he considered that there were many faults in the structure. He suggests that Shakespeare used an outmoded structural technique in order to allow the audience to focus on the language, poetry and imagery of the play:

> Why is his dramatic technique crude and apparently incoherent? The technique of *The Winter's Tale* is commonly regarded as deficient on a number of counts. First there is that awkward gap of sixteen years between the two parts of the play . . . and there is a patch of astonishingly awkward management towards the end of Act IV scene iv, beginning at the point where Camillo questions Florizel and learns that he is determined to 'put to sea' with Perdita.

Elsewhere, Bethell wrote of Shakespeare that 'having to skip sixteen years after Act 3, he desperately drags in Father Time with an hourglass'. But Nevill Coghill, writing ten years later, takes each of Bethell's points that criticise Shakespeare's structuring of *The Winter's Tale* and argues convincingly against them. Coghill's detailed argument concludes: 'There is nothing antiquated or otiose in stagecraft such as this.'

Other critics similarly provided strong justification of the play's artistic and aesthetic qualities. In 1947, G Wilson Knight defended the structure of *The Winter's Tale*. He feels that it displayed a balanced contrast between 'sinful maturity and nature-guarded youth in close association with seasonal change'. Wilson Knight suggests that 'In Leontes Shakespeare's tragic art has reached a new compactness and intensity . . . far from relaxing, Shakespeare's art is, on every front advancing'.

In a similarly positive appraisal, E M W Tillyard judged *The Winter's Tale* to be one of Shakespeare's most significant plays, claiming that it 'presented the whole tragic pattern, from prosperity to destruction, regeneration, and still fairer prosperity, in full view of the audience'. Tillyard felt that there was 'No blurring, but clean contrast. The paranoiac world of Leontes is set against the everyday world of the courtiers and the world, still of everyday but intensified, of Hermione. Leontes' world is marvellously expressed by the hot and twisted language he uses.' He particularly admired Act 4 Scene 4, though he criticised the way that many productions played it:

> It has been far too much the property of vague young women doing eurhythmics at Speech Days or on vicarage lawns; and, when it is acted professionally, the part of Perdita is usually taken by some pretty little fool or pert suburban charmer.

Tillyard considered that Perdita 'is one of Shakespeare's richest characters; at once a symbol and a human being'. He describes her as the embodiment of 'original virtue', as opposed to Iago (in *Othello*) whom he described as embodying 'original sin'. Praising the structural contrast of Bohemia with Sicilia Tillyard felt that Shakespeare gave the 'country life . . . the fullest force of actuality . . . the whole country setting stands out as the cleanest and most elegant symbol of the new life into which the old horrors are to be transmuted'.

Inga-Stina Ewbank, writing in 1964, discusses Shakespeare's use of time as a theme throughout the play. She defends the use of Time as a dramatic figure in the play, and responds to many of the criticisms of the structural pattern of *The Winter's Tale*. By relating the theme of time in *The Winter's Tale* to the *Sonnets*, Ewbank persuasively argues that time is 'intensely present as a controlling and shaping figure behind the dramatic structure and technique'. She particularly focuses on the length of time taken by the action of the play, refuting the earlier criticism of Shakespeare's construction of the play, particularly that made by Bethell:

> Not only does the action span a long period, so as – and this never happens in the tragedies – to give working-space to time, both as Revealer and as Destroyer; but, through the arrangement of the play into two halves separated by the

'wide gap' of sixteen years, past and present can be emphatically juxtaposed. The structure thus becomes a vehicle for the exploration of the meanings of time – in the sense of what time does to man.

Ewbank identifies the direct and indirect references to time throughout the play, and comments that 'the structure of events is shaped so as to give the impression that Leontes has not once stopped to think'. Using the ever-slippery 'we' (see page 87), she writes that, 'If we have been aware of the insistence on, and the importance of, the time theme in the first half of the play, we are, I think, prepared to see the introduction of Father Time here as more than a mere stop-gap, a desperate attempt to tidy over the Romance breach of the unities.' For Ewbank, the figure of Time is 'a concrete image of the multiplicity which the play as a whole dramatises and which is a leading theme of the second half of the play'.

Examining the final scene, Ewbank relates the theme of time to Shakespeare's *Sonnets*, asserting that 'Hermione's return represents another form of victory over time; she is a living proof that "Love's not Time's fool, though rosy lips and cheeks / Within his bending sickle's compass come" (*Sonnet 116*)'. Ewbank concludes, 'These sonnet lines could perhaps also paraphrase the truth that time has finally revealed to Leontes: paradoxically, time has at last in its triumph brought about its own defeat'.

The growing critical estimation accorded to *The Winter's Tale* is also evident in Derek Traversi's *Shakespeare: The Last Phase*, 1954. Traversi acknowledges it as one of Shakespeare's greatest plays:

> To pass from *Pericles* and *Cymbeline* to *The Winter's Tale* is to leave the field of experiment for that of finished achievement. In this play, in fact, the symbolic conception of drama that characterises Shakespeare's final period attains its first, and possibly its most assured success.

Traversi uses a comparison with music to analyse what he considers to be the four movements of the play. The opening tragic movement follows the breakdown of the unity between the central characters, which concludes with the casting out of Perdita to the elements, followed by the anger of Apollo. The second movement is the tempest, which continues the idea of the anger of Apollo, and the discovery of Perdita by the Shepherd. It unites the ideas of birth and death and links the tragic past to the happier times to come. The third movement is the pastoral scene, which establishes the love of Perdita and Florizel. The anger of Polixenes unites the two fathers and the two halves of the play. The fourth movement

> completes the balanced structure of the play by introducing with full effect the idea of penitence as prelude to restoration, by consummating the marriage of the two children and by achieving, through them, the reconciliation of their respective parents and the 'resurrection' of Hermione in all her gracious perfection. The rhythm of human experience, thus attuned to that of the seasons in their successive course, is rounded off in an inclusive harmony.

Traversi lays much stress on the first scene's references to the friendship of Polixenes and Leontes, and the ambiguous images of growth and of division. He claims that time is important from the beginning of the play as Polixenes looks back to an idyll which seemed timeless. This innocence is lost when the two kings grow up and 'stronger blood' or sexual awareness becomes dominant in their lives. Traversi sees this as ironic as the development of sexual maturity also leads to Leontes' conviction that Polixenes has betrayed him with Hermione. Traversi also focuses on the antitheses and dislocation in the language of *The Winter's Tale*, and on the double meanings carried by many of the key words in the first three acts of the play. A typical example of this style is revealed in his comment on the following four lines:

> This entertainment
> May a free face put on, derive a liberty
> From heartiness, from bounty, fertile bosom,
> And well become the agent   *(Act 1 Scene 2, lines 111–14)*

> 'Entertainment', 'free', 'liberty', 'fertile' are all words capable in themselves of a positive, healthy interpretation but, in the mind of the speaker, freedom is associated with prodigality and liberty with licence, whilst fertility itself appears as the overflow of wantonness.

F R Leavis speaks of *The Winter's Tale* in *The Common Pursuit* (1965) as a 'supreme instance of Shakespeare's poetic complexity – of the impossibility, if one is to speak with any relevance of the play, of considering character, episode, theme, and plot in abstraction from the local effects, inexhaustibly subtle in their inter-play, of the poetry, and from the larger symbolic effects to which these give life'. He feels that the play is 'not romantically licentious, or loose in organisation, or indulgent in a fairy-tale way to human fondness'. In contrast to many earlier critics, he rejects the psychological analysis of character, and concentrates on the relationship between character, speech and themes, claiming that

> so large a part of the function of the words spoken by
> the characters is so plainly something other than to
> 'create' the speakers, or to advance an action that can
> profitably be considered in terms of the interacting of
> individuals.

Caroline Spurgeon opened up a further critical perspective on *The Winter's Tale*: the study of its imagery. In *Shakespeare's Imagery and What it Tells Us*, she identifies what she feels to be the dominant image pattern in *The Winter's Tale*:

> The common flow of life through all things, in nature and man
> alike, seen in the sap rising in the tree, the habits and character
> of the flowers, the result of the marriage of base and noble
> stock, whether it be of roses or human beings, the emotions of
> birds, animals and men, the working of the poison of disease
> alike in mind and in body, the curative power, the tonic
> 'medicine' of a gay or honest presence, and above all, the
> oneness of rhythm, of law of movement, in the human body
> and human emotions with the great fundamental rhythmical
> movements of nature herself.
> More in this play than anywhere else is the ebb and flow of
> emotion exquisitely mirrored in the ebb and flow of blood in
> the face, obeying, as it does, the same laws, and responding to
> the same inner stimulus. 'I'll blush you thanks', cries Perdita to
> Camillo.
> And, above all, it is perfectly and exquisitely in keeping

with this central imaginative idea, that Florizel, in the height of his emotion and adoration of the beauty and wild natural grace of Perdita, should see the poetry of the motion of her young body as a part of the ordered and rhythmic flow of nature herself in the movement of the tides, and would have her stay for every part of that larger movement, so that he cries in ecstasy,

> When you do dance, I wish you
> A wave o'th'sea, that you might ever do
> Nothing but that   (Act 4 Scene 4, lines 140–2)

It should be noted that although the value of Caroline Spurgeon's pioneering study of Shakespeare's imagery has been acknowledged by later critics, her work has also been much criticised. For example, she underestimates the amount of imagery in *The Winter's Tale* and only occasionally examines how the imagery relates to the dramatic context of the play. She has also been criticised for her flowery style and her invariable tone of praise, avoiding any critical appraisal of the play's imagery. In this she echoes the 'bardolatry' that has dogged Shakespeare criticism ever since the Romantics of the early nineteenth century. Notwithstanding such flaws, her work is immensely valuable in encouraging the study of imagery, which is such a distinctive feature of every Shakespeare play.

M M Mahood's work on Shakespeare's use of imagery and puns is also very illuminating. Her book *Shakespeare's Wordplay* contains a fascinating chapter on wordplay in *The Winter's Tale*. You can find more on imagery in the Language section, and on page 112.

Modern criticism

Throughout the second half of the twentieth century and in the twenty-first, critical approaches to Shakespeare have radically challenged the style and assumptions of the traditional approaches described above. New critical approaches argue that traditional interpretations, with their focus on character and personal feelings, are individualistic and misleading; they ignore society and history, and so divorce literary, dramatic and aesthetic matters from their social context; further, their detachment from the real world makes them elitist, sexist and unpolitical.

Modern critical perspectives therefore shift the focus from studying characters as individuals to how social conditions (of the world of the play and of Shakespeare's England) are reflected in characters' relationships, language and behaviour. Modern criticism also concerns itself with how changing social assumptions at different periods of time have affected interpretations of the play.

It is significant, however, to note that *The Winter's Tale* has attracted less radical critical attention than the 'romance' that followed it, *The Tempest* (see below). As will be shown, although the play has generated a good deal of modern criticism (particularly feminist), 'political' approaches to the play are rare. There appears to be a good deal of continuity between modern and traditional criticism, for example in identifying the Jacobean contexts and relevances of the play, and in performance criticism (see pages 52, 102–4). That continuity is evident in T G Bishop's *Shakespeare and the Theatre of Wonder*, 1996. Bishop uses 'wonder' as a way of understanding the play, showing that it is a key component of Shakespeare's method of exploring social and psychological aspects of *The Winter's Tale*.

The following discussion is organised under headings which represent major contemporary critical perspectives (political, feminist, performance, psychoanalytic, postmodern). But it is vital to appreciate that there is often overlap between the categories, and that to pigeonhole any example of criticism too precisely is to reduce its value and application.

Political criticism

'Political criticism' is a convenient label for approaches concerned with power and social structure in the world of the play, in Shakespeare's time and in our own. *The Winter's Tale* appears to be resistant to such interpretations, being centrally concerned with such matters as the cycle of seasonal change, birth and death, repentance and regeneration. As Harold Bloom caustically remarked in 1999:

> Ideologues do not cluster around *The Winter's Tale*, as they do *The Tempest*, so neither performance nor commentary is much politicised, even in these bad days.

Bloom's 'bad days' indicates his detestation of much modern criticism, and he is correct in noting that *The Tempest* has attracted much political criticism, but the identification is unsurprising, because that play (unlike *The Winter's Tale*) directly raises issues of colonialism, racism, government, power and state. At the most obvious level, *The Tempest* invites the fraught political question 'To whom does the island belong?' In contrast, *The Winter's Tale* seems more concerned with the fairy-tale aspects of romance, with personal relationships and feelings, with the corrosive effects of paranoia and sexual jealousy. The leading Shakespeare scholar Stanley Wells acknowledges this in his *Shakespeare: A Dramatic Life* as he discusses the play's ending. He sees not political but personal consequences, triggered by natural and individual actions:

> Here there are no macroscopic implications. Emphasis is placed not on the group but on individuals whose suffering we have followed closely; the focus is upon a few figures in their newly poised adjustments to each other, stressing the importance of human relationships as bulwarks against the forces of disaster – storm and tempest, both external and internal.

The play therefore seems not readily to invite questions of rule or power in Sicilia or Bohemia at levels which have implications for the state. Nonetheless, it is possible to identify certain features of both criticism and stage productions which have attempted to highlight 'political' aspects:

- Autolycus as representing the stability-threatening 'masterless man' of Elizabethan and Jacobean society.
- The Shepherd as representative of the Elizabethan and Jacobean enclosers of common land whose greed impoverished the labouring class.
- The intrusion of economics into the traditionally viewed ideal pastoral world (the Shepherd and the Clown have made sufficient surplus to be able to purchase imported goods on the open market).
- Time's claim to 'make stale / The glistering of this present' (Act 4 Scene 1), claimed by Russ McDonald in *The Bedford Companion to Shakespeare*, 1996, as perhaps having a particularly chilling effect on the sophisticated Blackfriars audience of 1610. Adorned in their most glittering clothing and jewelry, having paid dearly for their

admission, and conscious of their superiority (whether social, political, or financial), the members of this crowd are warned that their days are numbered, that the darlings of fashion are always supplanted by others who are wealthier, more beautiful, more powerful.

- Perdita's words about Polixenes as a criticism of monarchy and hierarchy, and as foreshadowing an egalitarian society:

> I was about to speak and tell him plainly
> The self-same sun that shines upon his court
> Hides not his visage from our cottage but
> Looks on alike.   (*Act 4 Scene 4, lines 422–5*)

Two well-known 'political' critics, Terry Eagleton and Jan Kott, have commented on aspects of the play. In discussing the apparent polarity between court and country, Eagleton focuses particularly on the nature/nurture exchange between Perdita and Polixenes (Act 4 Scene 4, lines 87–97). In a difficult passage he uses it to suggest that

> Nature itself produces the means of its own transformation, contains that which goes beyond it. What goes beyond it – art, civilisation, culture, language, love – is thus no mere external 'supplement' to it, but is internal to its very design. If Nature is always cultural, then a particular culture can always be seen as natural. Those forms of surplus are legitimate which have their roots in the very natural order they transcend, and which provides the source of that transcendence.

Eagleton's argument is that in *The Winter's Tale* Shakespeare suggests the difference in class and status are 'natural, because somehow produced by Nature'. He says that all human beings, despite their social rank, share human nature, 'yet this shared nature is refined by civilised breeding beyond itself, generating hierarchical differences which none the less retain roots in a common soil'.

The Polish critic Jan Kott is best known for his book *Shakespeare Our Contemporary* (1965). Kott fought with the Polish army and underground movement against the Nazis in the Second World War (1939–45), and had direct experience of the suffering and terror caused by Stalinist repression in Poland in the years after the war.

Kott's book draws parallels between the violence and cruelty of the modern world and the worlds of tyranny and despair that Shakespeare depicted in his tragedies. Kott does not discuss *The Winter's Tale* in his book, but in a discussion on theatre with Charles Marowitz (published in *Recycling Shakespeare*) in the 1980s, Kott says that he feels that some of Shakespeare's plays 'have taken on a new relevance for modern audiences. *The Winter's Tale* . . . has, in the past ten years or so, begun to carry a new message and a new fascination; probably because of a new temporal attitude which has developed in regard to Shakespeare. There is some obscurity or darkness in this play which has now become dazzling and tempting.' Unfortunately Kott does not define his view of either the 'darkness' or how he feels that it has now become 'dazzling'.

This section concludes with the observation that the most obvious 'political' interpretation might seem to arise from Leontes being called a 'tyrant'. But the play shows that his tyranny is exercised over his family, rather than Sicilia. It is this patriarchal aspect of the play that has generated much vigorous argument, as the following discussion of feminist criticism demonstrates.

Feminist criticism

Feminist criticism is part of the wider project of feminism, which aims to achieve rights and equality for women in social, political and economic life. It challenges sexism: those beliefs and practices which result in the degradation, oppression and subordination of women. Feminist criticism therefore challenges traditional portrayals of women characters as examples of 'virtue' or 'vice'. It rejects 'male ownership' of criticism in which men determine what questions are to be asked of a play, and which answers are acceptable. Feminism argues that male criticism often neglects, represses or misrepresents female experience, and stereotypes or distorts women's points of view.

The feminist critics of *The Winter's Tale* tend to divide broadly into two main camps. One, represented by Juliet Dusinberre and Marilyn French, suggests that Shakespeare challenges some of the conventional seventeenth-century views of women. This view claims that though women are treated as property and are subject to a masculine social system, by presenting this on the stage Shakespeare is making a positive point about women. In her introduction to the second edition of *Shakespeare and the Nature of Women*, Dusinberre draws attention to the fact that women on the Shakespearean stage were an artificial construct of a creature called 'woman', being played either by a boy or possibly an adult man. Dusinberre points out that Hermione is blamed by Polixenes, even if with excessively polite humour, for the loss of his own and Leontes' innocence:

> O my most sacred lady,
> Temptations have since then been born to's: for
> In those unfledged days was my wife a girl;
> Your precious self had then not crossed the eyes
> Of my young playfellow.   (Act 1 Scene 2, lines 76–80)

Hermione rejects this view of sin in favour of the virtue of constancy:

> If you first sinned with us, and that with us
> You did continue fault, and that you slipped not
> With any but with us.   (Act 1 Scene 2, lines 84–6)

Leontes' accusation takes away Hermione's status. She is treated like a common criminal, dragged to a public trial. Dusinberre makes the point that, 'A man who is unchaste loses nothing in the eyes of the world. A woman who is unchaste is nothing . . . A woman's chastity included all other virtues'. Hermione can offer no defence of her innocence because she has no identity apart from the chastity which has been discredited:

> Since what I am to say must be but that
> Which contradicts my accusation, and
> The testimony on my part no other
> But what comes from myself, it shall scarce boot me
> To say 'Not guilty'. Mine integrity,
> Being counted falsehood, shall, as I express it,
> Be so received.   (Act 3 Scene 2, lines 20–6)

Dusinberre suggests that Antigonus shares the commonly held masculine view that women must be controlled, and he speaks of the drastic step of gelding his own daughters. For Antigonus, the loss of Hermione's chastity implicates that of his wife and daughters – even all women:

For every inch of woman in the world,
Ay, every dram of woman's flesh is false,
If she be.   *(Act 2 Scene 1, lines 137–9)*

Dusinberre praises Paulina for sticking to her view of right and wrong independently of her husband. When Leontes taunts Antigonus, 'What? Canst not rule her?', Paulina immediately reposts:

From all dishonesty he can. In this,
Unless he take the course that you have done –
Commit me for committing honour – trust it,
He shall not rule me.   *(Act 2 Scene 3, lines 47–50)*

As Dusinberre points out, the eloquence of Hermione and Paulina contrasts with the cowardly silence of Leontes' courtiers. She also praises Shakespeare for debunking the idea of making women into goddesses by letting Hermione grow realistically older:

Hermione was not so much wrinkled, nothing
So agèd as this seems.   *(Act 5 Scene 3, lines 28–9)*

Lisa Jardine and Valerie Traub, among others, argue an alternative feminist view; that the play does not challenge conventional male perspectives, but upholds them. Traub sums up this view: 'Shakespeare . . . perpetuates the defensive structures of dominance instituted by men.' Traub's starting point is her assumption that it is 'a commonplace that Shakespeare was preoccupied with the uncontrollability of women's sexuality'. She claims that 'all the men in Leontes' court depend on sexual dualism to mediate their relations with women'. Polixenes blames women for his fall from innocence, Antigonus will 'geld' his daughters, and Leontes believes that 'many a man' has been cuckolded. Hermione has to be killed in order to restore his peace:

say that she were gone,
Given to the fire, a moiety of my rest
Might come to me again.   *(Act 2 Scene 3, lines 7–9)*

For Traub, and other feminists holding this viewpoint, Hermione is an 'offering made in hope of reconstituting Leontes' sacred feminine ideal'. However, at the end of the play, Hermione becomes a statue brought to life, now 'warm not hot'. She is silent, apart from one speech made to her daughter, in contrast to her earlier articulacy. That silence confirms the male view of what a woman should be. Leontes regains his virtuous wife and control over social relations 'integrating the two remaining isolated figures, Paulina and Camillo'.

It is valuable to note that feminist criticism is not written solely by female critics. For example, Richard Wilson asserts that Shakespeare's late plays expose the attempt by males in the Jacobean period to gain control over what had been considered women's matters: conception, pregnancy and childbirth (for example as doctors began to supervise midwives). The implication is that Leontes' obsessive imaginings of Hermione's infidelity reflect Jacobean male anxiety about whether their children really were their own.

Such readings (like all critical interpretations) raise the question of whether they are what Shakespeare intended. Was he purposefully challenging female stereotyping imposed by men? Whilst many critics today argue that Shakespeare's intentions can never be known, a distinctive feature of feminist criticism is that it subjects *The Winter's Tale* (and all Shakespeare's plays) to critical scrutiny, exposing patriarchal conventions as irrational and repressive.

Performance criticism

Performance criticism fully acknowledges that *The Winter's Tale* is a play: a script to be performed by actors to an audience. It examines all aspects of the play in performance: its staging in the theatre or on film and video. Performance criticism focuses on Shakespeare's stagecraft and the semiotics of theatre (words, costumes, gestures, etc.), together with the 'afterlife' of the play (what happened to *The Winter's Tale* after Shakespeare wrote it). That involves scrutiny of how productions at different periods have presented the play, and how the text has been cut, added to, rewritten and rearranged to present a version felt appropriate to the times.

The Winter's Tale was popular in Shakespeare's own time. It was chosen to be part of the celebrations for the marriage feast of the Princess Elizabeth in 1613, and records suggest that it was performed frequently, more often than *King Lear*, for example. Since then, each successive age has taken from *The Winter's Tale* what it found relevant and adapted the play to suit its own taste. In some ways the practical criticism of the director can be of equal interest to that of the scholar.

During the eighteenth century *The Winter's Tale* fell out of favour. Alexander Pope suggested that Shakespeare could not have written it because it had too many improbabilities and flouted the traditional unities of time, place and action. Some directors rewrote much of the play, and one even renamed it *The Sheep-shearing Or Florizel and Perdita*, abandoning the tragic scenes altogether.

With the growing influence of Romanticism in the early and mid-nineteenth century, *The Winter's Tale* became more popular and was praised for its realism. Much more stress was laid on the jealous passion of Leontes and on the reconciliation at the end. There is a story that one actor playing Leontes, Macready, frightened his leading lady, Helen Faucit, with his passionate emotion in the statue scene.

Late in the nineteenth century, Charles Kean's production stressed a kind of historical realism – something that Shakespeare had ignored. Having chosen his era, Ancient Greece, Kean cut everything that did not fit with that time, and set the play in Syracuse and Bythnia (Bythnia because it has a sea-coast, unlike Bohemia). As Queen Victoria attended the production, Kean also cut everything remotely indelicate, even lines such as 'The queen your mother rounds apace'. To exemplify the sophistication of Leontes' court, Kean also added a dance performed by 'three dozen ladies of the corps de ballet, attired in glittering armour as youthful warriors' in Act 1 Scene 2. The sets and costumes were elaborate and one critic commented that there 'must have been three hundred persons engaged in the sheep-shearing festival'. At about the same time, Burton in America appears to have staged a version closer to Shakespeare's script but heavily influenced by Kean's use of spectacle.

During the late nineteenth century, *The Winter's Tale* was frequently acted and was very popular. In the early part of the twentieth century, Max Beerbohm Tree produced a version which savagely cut the original script. He reduced it to three acts by cutting all possible sexual references, and expanded the action of what he had left by including lots of stage business and even a country cottage by a real stream for Perdita. The first production to use a full version of the script again was the 1912 production by Howard Granville-Barker. He used a set which was non-representational and suggested location, rather than trying to create it naturalistically on stage. He also used the most modern kind of lighting and re-established the use of the apron stage, taking the actors closer to the audience.

In the latter half of the twentieth century there was a growing emphasis on analysing the language from the point of view of an actor. Searching for the rhythms of the verse and prose, and exploring how to speak the text, is very revealing. Cicely Berry in *The Actor and the Text* offers valuable insight into how an actor might approach some of the major speeches in *The Winter's Tale*. In the Players of Shakespeare series there are fascinating accounts from the actors' points of view. These include Gemma Jones' account of her search for Hermione's character when she was playing in *The Winter's Tale* for the Royal Shakespeare Company, and Richard McCabe's discussion of his playing of Autolycus.

Many modern productions stress the horror of Leontes' state of mind; his wilful self-deception and cruelty to Hermione. Some productions, such as Nicholas Hytner's National Theatre production in 2001, reject the idea of a neat and tidy reconciliation at the end of the play, preferring a much more problematic resolution of the conflicts. In this production, although Hermione briefly put her arms around Leontes' neck on the line, 'She embraces him', she embraced Perdita much more warmly and mother and daughter stayed entwined in the final spotlight after the other characters had left the stage. Leontes' pairing of Camillo and Paulina did not seem to be to the taste of either. Leontes left the stage with Paulina, Polixenes with Camillo, with Florizel looking back at Perdita as he left.

Psychoanalytic criticism

In the twentieth century, psychoanalysis became a major influence on the understanding and interpretation of human behaviour. The founder of psychoanalysis, Sigmund Freud, explained personality as the result of unconscious and irrational desires, repressed memories or wishes, sexuality, fantasy, anxiety and conflict. Freud's theories have had a strong influence on criticism and stagings of Shakespeare's plays, most obviously on *Hamlet* in the well-known claim that Hamlet suffers from an Oedipus complex.

A tendency of psychoanalytic criticism is to observe that the ferocity of Leontes' jealousy is increased by the fact that Hermione's supposed adultery is with his friend. Such criticism concentrates on the opening scene's emphasis on the close boyhood friendship of Leontes and

Polixenes. This interpretation offers a reading of the play which makes Polixenes the great love of Leontes' life, and therefore also the source of his greatest guilt. Leontes is unconsciously transferring his own love for Polixenes onto Hermione and blames her with an intensity commensurate with his own hidden guilty feelings.

Murray M Schwartz is probably representative of a radical psychoanalytic reading. He imposes a Freudian reading on Leontes' jealousy. He feels that the childhood friendship of Leontes and Polixenes is similar to the 'narcissistic and idealised' relationship between mother and son. Schwartz sees the name of Mamillius (associated with the idea of a lactating breast) as symbolic, a confirmation that Leontes' 'masculine image of himself is maternally fixated'. Though such theories may seem far-fetched, Schwartz makes the thought-provoking point that the four older men in the play share certain extreme attitudes towards women; that they can only be either 'sacred' or 'temptations'.

Writing in 1994, B J Sokol also discusses *The Winter's Tale* from a psychoanalytic perspective. He applies Freudian theories to the themes of art and illusion in the play and concentrates a large proportion of his work on the real Giulio (Julio) Romano and his explicitly sexual etchings. His theory seems to be that there was some unconscious sexual motive behind Shakespeare's choice of sculptor (or painter) of Hermione's statue.

Such interpretations reveal the obvious weaknesses in applying psychoanalytic theories to *The Winter's Tale*. They are highly speculative, and can be neither proved nor disproved. Psychoanalytic approaches are therefore often accused of imposing interpretations based on theory rather than upon Shakespeare's text. Nonetheless, the play has obvious features which seem to invite psychoanalytic approaches: fantasy and imagination, instability of language, obsessive emotions, sexual jealousy, cruelty and a bizarre death (Antigonus eaten by the bear), tortured dreams, fractured family relationships and an evident desire for wish-fulfilment in reuniting families and bringing the dead back to life.

Postmodern criticism

Postmodern criticism (sometimes called 'deconstruction') is not always easy to understand because it is not centrally concerned with consistency or reasoned argument. It does not accept that one section of the story is necessarily connected to what follows, or that characters relate to each other in meaningful ways. Because of such assumptions, postmodern criticism is sometimes described as 'reading against the grain' or, less politely, as 'textual harassment'. The approach therefore has obvious drawbacks in providing a model for examination students who are expected to display reasoned, coherent argument, and respect for the evidence of the text.

Postmodern approaches to *The Winter's Tale* are most clearly seen in stage productions. There, you could think of it as simply 'a mixture of styles'. The label 'postmodern' is applied to productions which self-consciously show little regard for consistency in character, or for coherence in telling the story. Characters are dressed in costumes from very different historical periods, and carry both modern and ancient weapons. Ironically, Shakespeare himself has been regarded as a postmodern writer in the way he mixes genres in his plays: comedy with tragedy, for example the death of Antigonus with the Clown's description of it.

Postmodernism often revels in the cleverness of its own use of language, and accepts all kinds of anomalies and contradictions in a spirit of playfulness or 'carnival'. It abandons any notion of the organic unity of the play, and rejects the assumption that *The Winter's Tale* possesses clear patterns or themes. Some postmodern critics even deny the possibility of finding meaning in language. They claim that words simply refer to other words, and so any interpretation is endlessly delayed (or 'deferred' as the deconstructionists say). Others focus on minor or marginal characters, or on loose ends, gaps or silences in the play, claiming that these features, often overlooked as unimportant, reveal significant truths about the play.

The language of postmodern criticism is often difficult to understand, making its advocates' arguments hard to follow. For example, Michael D Bristol claims that part of the early tragedy in *The Winter's Tale* comes from the contrast between 'the empty and atemporal internal content of certain characters and the abundantly concretised spatiotemporal environment they inhabit'. Such language compounds the difficulty of following the argument of a postmodern critic. Bristol discusses *The Winter's Tale* in terms of a gift economy. He assumes that Polixenes and Leontes are engaged in rivalry to exceed each other in gift giving, 'a bitter and deadly struggle for honour and prestige'. He infers that Leontes refuses to visit Bohemia, and by an analysis of their names (Leontes = Leo, sun/summer, Polixenes = polus, the North Star) concludes that this refusal signifies 'a literally catastrophic derangement of temporal and cosmological order'.

Another example of postmodern criticism is Simon Palfrey's *Late Shakespeare: A New World of Words*, 1997. Palfrey's postmodern style has echoes of psychoanalytic criticism. He draws attention to Autolycus' ballad of the woman turned into a 'cold fish for she would not exchange flesh with one that loved her', and says that this is what Leontes 'apparently does to his "too hot" wife'. Hermione becomes a cold statue. But Palfrey's judgement of Autolycus, calling him, 'the new god of the age, turning full circle into a tyranny as emasculating, and perhaps as silencing, as Leontes', again displays the eclecticism of the postmodern approach. It hints at, but does not clearly embrace, a political criticism which places Shakespeare's plays in the context of their times:

> Traditional festivity, like its pastoral cousin, cannot be fenced off from surrounding climes. In Shakespearian romance, the 'posterns' have been opened, and a tempestuous new world comes rushing in.

Organising your responses

The purpose of this section is to help you improve your writing about *The Winter's Tale*. It offers practical guidance on two kinds of tasks: writing about an extract from the play and writing an essay. Whether you are answering an examination question, preparing coursework (term papers), or carrying out research into your own chosen topic, this section will help you organise and present your responses.

Writing about an extract

It is an expected part of all Shakespeare study that you should be able to write well about an extract (sometimes called a 'passage') from the play. An extract is usually between 30 and 70 lines long, and you are invited to comment on it. The instructions vary. Sometimes the task is very briefly expressed:

- Write a detailed commentary on the following passage.
- Write about the effect of the extract on your own thoughts and feelings.

At other times a particular focus is specified for your writing:

- With close reference to the language and imagery of the passage, show in what ways it helps to establish important issues in the play.
- Analyse the style and structure of the extract, showing what it contributes to your appreciation of the play's major concerns.

In writing your response, you must of course take account of the precise wording of the task, and ensure you concentrate on each particular point specified. But however the invitation to write about an extract is expressed, it requires you to comment in detail on the language. You should identify and evaluate how the language may offer hints to an actor concerning the building of personality, contributes to plot development, offers opportunities for dramatic effect, and embodies crucial concerns of the play.

The following framework is a guide to how you can write a detailed commentary on an extract. Writing a paragraph on each item will help you bring out the meaning and significance of the extract, and show how Shakespeare achieves his effects.

Paragraph 1: Locate the extract in the play and say who is on stage.
Paragraph 2: State what the extract is about and identify its structure.
Paragraph 3: Identify the mood or atmosphere of the extract.
Paragraphs 4–8:

Diction (vocabulary)
Imagery
Antithesis
Repetition
Lists

} These paragraphs analyse how Shakespeare achieves his effects. They concentrate on the language of the extract, showing the dramatic effect of each item, and how the language expresses crucial concerns of the play.

Paragraph 9: Staging opportunities
Paragraph 10: Conclusion

The following example uses the framework to show how the paragraphs making up the essay might be written. The framework headings (in bold) would not, of course, appear in your essay. They are presented only to help you see how the framework is used.

Extract

POLIXENES   What means Sicilia?
HERMIONE   He something seems unsettled.
POLIXENES   How, my lord?
LEONTES   What cheer? How is't with you, best brother?
HERMIONE   You look
    As if you held a brow of much distraction.
    Are you moved, my lord?
LEONTES   No, in good earnest.   5
    How sometimes nature will betray its folly,
    Its tenderness, and make itself a pastime
    To harder bosoms! Looking on the lines
    Of my boy's face, methoughts I did recoil
    Twenty-three years, and saw myself unbreeched,   10
    In my green velvet coat; my dagger muzzled,
    Lest it should bite its master and so prove,
    As ornaments oft do, too dangerous.
    How like, methought, I then was to this kernel,
    This squash, this gentleman. Mine honest friend,   15

Will you take eggs for money?

MAMILLIUS   No, my lord, I'll fight.

LEONTES   You will? Why, happy man be's dole! My brother,
    Are you so fond of your young prince as we
    Do seem to be of ours?

POLIXENES   If at home, sir   20
    He's all my exercise, my mirth, my matter;
    Now my sworn friend, and then mine enemy;
    My parasite, my soldier, statesman, all.
    He makes a July's day short as December,
    And with his varying childness cures in me   25
    Thoughts that would thick my blood.

LEONTES   So stands this squire
    Officed with me. We two will walk, my lord,
    And leave you to your graver steps. Hermione,
    How thou lov'st us show in our brother's welcome.
    Let what is dear in Sicily be cheap.   30
    Next to thyself and my young rover, he's
    Apparent to my heart.

HERMIONE   If you would seek us,
    We are yours i'th' garden. Shall's attend you there?

LEONTES   To your own bents dispose you; you'll be found,
    Be you beneath the sky. [*Aside*] I am angling now,   35
    Though you perceive me not how I give line.
    Go to, go to!
    How she holds up the neb, the bill to him!
    And arms her with the boldness of a wife
    To her allowing husband!
          [*Exeunt Polixenes, Hermione, and Attendants*]
          Gone already!   40
    Inch-thick, knee-deep, o'er head and ears a forked one!
    Go play, boy, play: thy mother plays, and I
    Play too – but so disgraced a part whose issue
    Will hiss me to my grave. Contempt and clamour
    Will be my knell. Go play, boy, play. There have been,   45
    Or I am much deceived, cuckolds ere now;
    And many a man there is, even at this present,
    Now, while I speak this, holds his wife by th'arm,
    That little thinks she has been sluiced in's absence,

And his pond fished by his next neighbour, by   50
Sir Smile, his neighbour. Nay, there's comfort in't
Whiles other men have gates, and those gates opened,
As mine, against their will. Should all despair
That have revolted wives, the tenth of mankind
Would hang themselves. Physic for't there's none: 55
It is a bawdy planet, that will strike
Where 'tis predominant; and 'tis powerful, think it,
From east, west, north and south. Be it concluded,
No barricado for a belly. Know't,
It will let in and out the enemy   60
With bag and baggage. Many thousand on's
Have the disease and feel't not. How now, boy!
MAMILLIUS   I am like you, they say.   *(Act 1 Scene 2, lines 146–208)*

Paragraph 1: Locate the extract in the play and say who is on stage.
This extract occurs just after Leontes' first shocking speeches about
his jealous suspicions concerning his wife and his friend. Hermione
and Polixenes and some attendants are also on stage but not in a
position to hear Leontes. Leontes has been speaking both directly to
Mamillius and to himself in language that reflects the emotional
turmoil he is experiencing. Polixenes and Hermione have noticed his
distress and come to join him.

Paragraph 2: State what the extract is about and identify its structure.
(Begin with one or two sentences identifying what the extract is about,
followed by several sentences briefly identifying its structure, that is,
the different sections of the extract.)

   The extract shows how quickly Leontes becomes convinced of the
adultery between his wife and his friend. At the beginning of the
extract Leontes is able to dissemble and to reply coherently and with
some irony to Polixenes and Hermione when they enquire what is
disturbing him. Thinking of Mamillius, he refers to memories of his
own childhood and speaks touchingly of what seems to have been a
favourite coat. He asks Polixenes about his son and Polixenes speaks
of his great affection for him. Leontes instructs Hermione to love
Polixenes. Hermione and Polixenes leave the stage with the
attendants. Though Mamillius is still present on stage and some of
Leontes' lines are directed to him, Leontes' speech seems like a

soliloquy, interrupted occasionally by Leontes' awareness of the presence of Mamillius. He is convinced of Hermione's adultery and tries to find comfort in thinking all women are sexually promiscuous.

Paragraph 3: Identify the mood or atmosphere of the extract.

The opening part of the extract is full of dramatic irony. The audience is aware of Leontes' suspicions but he conceals them from Hermione and Polixenes. It is also ironic when Leontes asks Mamillius whether he would be easily fooled: 'Will you take eggs for money?' There is an ominous note of warning when Leontes says: 'you'll be found, / Be you beneath the sky'. Once Hermione and Polixenes have left the stage the mood is one of intense and savage jealousy.

Paragraph 4: Diction (vocabulary)

The language powerfully conveys dramatic irony. Polixenes comments that Leontes 'something seems unsettled'; an understatement for Leontes' feelings. Hermione says that he looks as though he 'held a brow of much distraction', which Leontes could interpret as a reference to the horns traditionally associated with a cuckold, to which he has previously referred when talking to Mamillius (lines 123–9). Leontes refers to the emotions evoked by the sight of his son, and his nostalgia for the innocence of his own childhood. The audience could interpret Leontes' feelings of being 'a pastime / To harder bosoms' as part of his sense of betrayal. The sound of many of the lines expresses Leontes' sexual disgust at Hermione's behaviour: 'she has been sluiced in's absence', or his anger: 'No barricado for a belly . . . bag and baggage'.

Paragraph 5: Imagery

Much of the first part of the extract is concerned with youth; of nostalgia for lost innocence, and the regenerative powers of the young. Leontes remembers the past with affection, recalling Polixenes' references to 'twinned lambs'. Polixenes says that the 'varying childness' of his son 'cures in me / Thoughts that would thick my blood' (make me feel old). Leontes uses animal imagery in relation to Hermione. He thinks of himself as a skilled fisherman 'angling', playing her on a 'line' and then sardonically: 'How she holds up the neb, the bill to him!' Leontes employs different meanings of the word 'play': his disgust at the thought of Hermione's adultery is expressed through the sexual coarseness of his imagery: 'sluiced', 'his pond fished', 'Sir Smile, his neighbour', 'No barricado for a belly'. Leontes' images also give an impression of the possession of women as property: 'Whiles other men have gates'. Here Shakespeare, reflecting the patriarchy of his time, gives a series of powerful images of a woman's body being no more than the possession of a man – an owned fishpond, exclusive to the man who owns it and prohibited to others. He reduces the idea of a woman to a 'belly', merely a vessel for his bloodline, which needs the protection of a barricade like a besieged city.

Paragraph 6: Antithesis
Through his use of antitheses Polixenes conveys the impression that his son is everything to him: 'Now my sworn friend, and then mine enemy . . . He makes a July's day short as December'. Ironically, Leontes' use of the opposition 'dear . . . cheap' expresses meaning contrary to his true intentions. It also carries the connotations of Hermione being 'dear' to him, but behaving as though she were 'cheap'. In his soliloquy Leontes puns antithetically on 'plays' and 'play', setting his fevered imaginings of Hermione's infidelity against his enforced role. The imagery that follows similarly brings out the opposition between a cuckolded man's sense of security and the adulterous behaviour of his wife.

Paragraph 7: Repetition
Most of the examples of repetition in this extract serve to intensify Leontes' sense of disgust and revulsion as he imagines the adultery between Polixenes and Hermione. He uses the word 'play' in various ways, shifting the definition to suit his intentions. He concludes the series of puns on 'play' with the idea of himself being forced to act a role (that of cuckold) which will bring 'Contempt and clamour' on him. There is a repetitive, almost jarring rhythm in the soliloquy, as the series of brief but intense thoughts succeed one another expressing his tortured state of his mind.

Paragraph 8: Lists
Two sets of lists in this extract concern the importance of the relationship between fathers and sons. Mamillius is described by Leontes as 'this kernel, / This squash, this gentleman' and Polixenes calls Florizel 'my exercise, my mirth, my matter' and 'My parasite, my

soldier, statesman, all'. The major list, though, is the series of images with which Leontes tries to comfort himself; 'There have been, / . . . cuckolds ere now'. The cumulative effect of this list, which finishes with 'Many thousand on's / Have the disease and feel't not', serves to reinforce the lack of consolation in the awareness that he is not alone in his jealousy; instead it intensifies the audience's sense of Leontes' pain.

Paragraph 9: Staging opportunities
This scene is set in a relatively public place. There have been attendants present as well as Leontes, Polixenes, Hermione, Camillo and Mamillius. The proxemics (relative positions on stage) have changed during this episode and are particularly effective in this extract, with opportunities for Polixenes and Hermione to observe Leontes, and Leontes to observe them. Visually striking is the presence of Mamillius as a symbol of innocence and a contrast to the diseased imagination of Leontes. In the section which deals with the expression of his jealousy, Shakespeare demonstrates his intention to involve the audience directly in Leontes' experience: 'many a man there is . . . / Now, while I speak this' and dramatic impact can be heightened when Leontes delivers the speech directly to the audience.

Paragraph 10: Conclusion
This extract focuses on the dramatic turning point between what Shakespeare has shown of the normality of Leontes' life: his love for his son, his wife and his friend; and the extent to which that normality is destroyed by his suspicions. Only the audience is aware of the way that Leontes is beginning to interpret everything he sees in the light of his jealous passion. It reveals the extent of Leontes' diseased imagination and his graphically expressed sexual torment. Shakespeare concentrates on the rapidity of the growth of Leontes' jealousy and the way that it distorts his view of everything around him. This will lead to the destruction of everything which he held dear at the beginning of the play.

Writing an essay
As part of your study of *The Winter's Tale* you will be asked to write essays, either under examination conditions or for coursework (term

papers). Examinations mean that you are under pressure of time, usually having around one hour to prepare and write each essay. Coursework means that you have much longer to think about and produce your essay. But whatever the type of essay, each will require you to develop an argument about a particular aspect of *The Winter's Tale*.

The people who read your essays (examiners, teachers, lecturers) will have certain expectations for your writing. They will know the play – you do not need to tell the story. In each essay they will expect you to discuss and analyse a particular topic, using evidence from the play to develop an argument in an organised, coherent and persuasive way. Examiners look for, and reward, what they call 'an informed personal response'. This simply means that you show you have good knowledge of the play ('informed') and can use evidence from it to support and justify your own viewpoint ('personal').

You can write about *The Winter's Tale* from different points of view. As pages 95–107 show, you can approach the play from a number of critical perspectives (feminist, political, psychoanalytic, etc.). You can also set the play in its social, literary, political and other contexts, as shown in the section on Contexts. You should write at different levels, moving beyond description to analysis and evaluation. Simply telling the story or describing characters is not as effective as analysing how events or characters embody wider concerns of the play – its themes, issues, preoccupations, or, more simply, 'what the play is about'. In *The Winter's Tale*, these wider concerns include friendship, jealousy, nature versus nurture and the pastoral genre.

How should you answer an examination question or write a coursework essay? The following threefold structure can help you organise your response:

opening paragraph
developing paragraphs
concluding paragraph.

Opening paragraph. Begin with a paragraph identifying what topic or issue you will focus on. Show that you have understood what the question is about. You probably will have prepared for particular topics. But look closely at the question and identify key words to see what particular aspect it asks you to write about. Adapt your material to answer that question. Examiners do not reward an essay, however well written, if it is not on the question set.

Developing paragraphs. This is the main body of your essay. In it, you develop your argument, point by point, paragraph by paragraph. Use evidence from the play that illuminates the topic or issue, and answers the question set. Each paragraph makes a point of dramatic or thematic significance. Some paragraphs could make points concerned with context or particular critical approaches. The effect of your argument builds up as each paragraph adds to the persuasive quality of your essay. Use brief quotations that support your argument, and show clearly just why they are relevant. Ensure that your essay demonstrates that you are aware that *The Winter's Tale* is a play; a drama intended for performance, and therefore open to a wide variety of interpretations and audience response.

Concluding paragraph. Your final paragraph pulls together your main conclusions. It does not simply repeat what you have written earlier, but summarises concisely how your essay has successfully answered the question.

Example

> Question: 'In spite of its painful emotions and events, *The Winter's Tale* is always recognisable as a comedy.' How far do you agree?

The following notes show the 'ingredients' of an answer. In an examination it is usually helpful to prepare similar notes from which you write your essay, paragraph by paragraph. To help you understand how contextual matters or points from different critical approaches might be included, the words 'Context' or 'Criticism' appear before some items. Remember that examiners are not impressed by 'name-dropping': use of critics' names. What they want you to show is your knowledge and judgement of the play and its contexts, and of how it has been interpreted from different critical perspectives.

Opening paragraph

Show that you understand why *The Winter's Tale* is classified as a comedy. (This has little to do with being funny. Comedy is a genre of drama and is the opposite of tragedy. In Shakespeare it usually involves a reconciliation and the apparent restoration of order and harmony.) You could argue that the first part of the play has all the elements of a tragedy. The question asks 'How far do you agree . . . ?' so you will need to justify your interpretation of the ending of the play, i.e. do you think that it ends 'happily', with the complete restoration of order and harmony?

Developing paragraphs

Now you should write a number of paragraphs on the 'painful emotions and events'. In each paragraph you should identify how you 'recognise' the potential for reconciliation and the restoration of harmony (or not). Some of the points that you could include are given below.

- Criticism: The sudden almost inexplicable onset of Leontes' jealousy – is the lack of explicit motive an indication that his mood will change again?
- Criticism: The concentration on the early close friendship of Polixenes and Leontes, as close as brothers – is there a suggestion that their friendship could be re-established? Is the suspected betrayal by Polixenes almost as painful as that of Hermione?
- The violence of Leontes' response to his suspicions – does the escape of Camillo and Polixenes suggest that there may be an opportunity for reconciliation? Is the hint of comedy in Paulina's robust rejection of Leontes' threats a signal for the audience?
- Context: The cruel and unjust treatment of Hermione.
- Does the message from the oracle suggest the potential for renewal in 'if that which is lost be not found'?
- Once the baby has been found, and the Shepherd and the Clown come on stage, does it seem certain that the end of the play will be comic?

- Context: Does the long pastoral scene establish the tone of joy in spite of Polixenes' threats?
- Context: Mamillius, Antigonus and the mariners all die.
- Criticism: Consider the genre of tragicomedy (a drama which combines both the subject matter and the forms of traditional tragedy and comedy).

Concluding paragraph
- Show that you understand that in literary and dramatic criticism 'comic' implies reconciliation and harmony at the end of a play, not necessarily humour.
- Do you feel that the pairing of Paulina and Camillo is dramatically apt?
- Do you feel that the restoration of Hermione is dramatically and thematically fulfilling?
- Indicate how far you feel that the ending of *The Winter's Tale* promises happiness and harmony for the characters, and for Bohemia and Sicily.

Writing about character

Much critical writing about *The Winter's Tale* traditionally focused on characters, writing about them as if they were living human beings. Today it is not sufficient just to describe their personalities. When you write about characters you will also be expected to show that they are dramatic constructs, part of Shakespeare's stagecraft. That means that they help suggest the wider concerns of the play, have certain dramatic functions, and are set in a social and political world with particular values and beliefs. They reflect and express issues of significance to Shakespeare's society – and today's.

All that may seem difficult and abstract. But don't feel overwhelmed. Everything you read in this book is written with those principles in mind, and can be a model for your own writing. Of course you should say what a character seems like to you, but you should also write about how Shakespeare makes him or her part of his overall dramatic design. For example:

- Camillo sets the scene in a prose conversation at the beginning of each 'half' of the play. He earns the role of trusted adviser to Leontes and to Polixenes.

- Camillo and Paulina each direct parts of the action of the play.
- Hermione is the focus of dramatic attention in a set-piece scene in both the tragic and the comic parts of the play. In Act 3 she is articulate, in Act 5 almost silent.

A different way of thinking of characters is that in Shakespeare's time, playwrights and audiences were less concerned with psychological realism than with character types and their functions. That is, they expected and recognised such stock figures of traditional drama as the scold (Paulina), the Clown, the cony-catcher (Autolycus), the young lovers from the pastoral genre (Florizel and Perdita). Today, film and television have accustomed audiences to expect the inner life of characters to be revealed. Although Shakespeare's characters do reveal thoughts and feelings, especially in soliloquy, his audiences tended to regard them as characters in a developing story, to be understood by how they formed part of that story, and by how far they conformed to certain well-known types and fulfilled certain traditional roles.

It can be helpful to think of minor characters, whose roles are little more than functional. They are dramatic devices who briefly perform their part, then disappear from the play. Archidamus seems to be of equal status to Camillo and contributes a great deal to Act 1 Scene 1. He helps to establish for the audience the comparative sophistication of the Sicilian court, the extent of the friendship of the two kings and the importance of Mamillius, but this dramatically important scene is his only contribution to the play. Emilia adds a powerful sense of female solidarity in the prison scene, though she is not named as a character appearing in any other scene. Mopsa and Dorcas have only a dozen or so lines and a song between them yet they can create a lasting impression on the audience of the vitality of the country life in Bohemia. They would have been familiar figures to a Jacobean audience. Cleomenes and Dion only appear in Act 3 Scene 1 and Act 5 Scene 1, but they play an important part in setting the reverent tone and atmosphere of faith in these scenes. Although actors playing these minor roles can create a vivid sense of personality, they exist only for certain particular dramatic purposes.

But there is also a danger in writing about the functions of characters or the character types they represent. To reduce a character to a mere plot device is just as inappropriate as treating him or her as a real person. In contrast with the minor characters, major characters have more extensive dramatic functions, and actors have far greater opportunities to create the stage illusion of a real person. When you write about characters in *The Winter's Tale* you should try to achieve a balance between analysing their personality, identifying the dilemmas they face, and placing them in their social, critical and dramatic contexts. That style of writing is found all through this Guide, and that, together with the following brief discussions, can help your own written responses to character.

Leontes' character has always posed problems for critics. There have been those who consider the suddenness of the onset of his jealousy as a flaw in the play. Others, including most modern critics, feel that this is entirely credible and psychologically realistic. Some even speak of Leontes being jealous from the opening of Act 1 Scene 2, pointing to the brevity of his speeches compared to the elaborate imagery of Polixenes. Dramatically the abruptness of his jealousy is striking, and the tortuous language with which he expresses his delusion mirrors the twisted emotions he is experiencing. With unconscious irony he rebukes Hermione, 'Your actions are my dreams.' His diseased imagination takes possession of all his senses, even to the point where he rejects the words of Apollo. His repentance is described by Cleomenes as 'saint-like', and he accepts Paulina's judgement. His simple response to the first touch of Hermione is emotionally poignant, 'O, she's warm!'

In several of his plays Shakespeare explores the causes and consequences of masculine jealousy. *Othello* is frequently compared to *The Winter's Tale* because the violence of Othello's reaction is echoed in the imagery used by Leontes. However there are profound differences between the two plays. In *Othello* the growth and development of Othello's jealousy occupies the major part of the play, and its causes are given as much prominence as the effects. The other play whose theme of jealousy is most frequently compared to *The Winter's Tale* is *Cymbeline*. In both *Othello* and *Cymbeline* the jealous passions are provoked and fostered by the villains of the plays: Iago and Iachimo. Only in *The Winter's Tale* does the jealousy arise from the self-deluding protagonist (the main character).

Jealousy is also a theme in Shakespeare's *Sonnets*. It is possible to interpret some of the sonnets as expressing Shakespeare's tortured feelings as he thinks about the relationship between his friend and his mistress; a situation which could be compared to the suspicions of

Leontes about Polixenes and Hermione.

In *The Winter's Tale* Shakespeare shows more graphically than anywhere else in his work the destructive effects of sexual jealousy, and it is important that the audience does not perceive the relationship between Hermione and Polixenes to be the actual cause of Leontes' jealousy. The audience watches Leontes talk himself into a passionate certainty even though he knows he has no absolute proof:

> That lacked sight only, nought for approbation
> But only seeing   *(Act 2 Scene 1, lines 177–8)*

When jealousy first strikes him, he moves rapidly from the conditional to absolute certainty:

>   This entertainment
> May a free face put on, derive a liberty
> From heartiness, from bounty, fertile bosom,
> And well become the agent   *(Act 1 Scene 2, lines 111–14)*

>   Then 'tis very credent
> Thou mayst co-join with something; and thou dost,
> And that beyond commission, and I find it,
> And that to the infection of my brains
> And hard'ning of my brows.   *(Act 1 Scene 2, lines 142–6)*

Leontes' jealousy leads him to reject everything he has valued, his friendship with Polixenes, his wife, even his faith in Apollo. Shakespeare makes it very clear that once he suspects Hermione, he feels that there is nothing in his life that he can rely on:

>   Is this nothing?
> Why then the world and all that's in't is nothing,
> The covering sky is nothing, Bohemia nothing,
> My wife is nothing, nor nothing have these nothings,
> If this be nothing.   *(Act 1 Scene 2, lines 292–5)*

Hermione was often seen as the ideal wife by early critics, who tended to concentrate particularly on her submission to the will of Leontes. Modern critics tend to see her as a woman whose lively and insistent persuasion of Polixenes leads her close to flirting with him. She is one of the few virtuous pregnant women in Shakespeare's plays and her momentary irritation with her importunate son is recognisable to all mothers (Act 2 Scene 1, lines 1–2). The audience is touched by the change from her maternal role, listening to the winter's tale 'Of sprites and goblins', to her dignified response to Leontes' public accusation. Her words, 'and so / The king's will be performed' are an echo of the biblical phrase, 'Thy will be done'. Hermione is innocent of any fault but always remains constant and obedient to her husband's will. Though some critics have called the role of Hermione weak and passive, this is not the experience of actors. Certainly she is not as aggressive and controlling as Paulina, but her dignity and quiet strength make her a powerful figure on stage. Hermione speaks with a lively confidence in her position as queen and mother in Act 1 and at the beginning of Act 2. After her accusation by Leontes, and in her trial she shows loyalty to Leontes in an articulate and measured defence which contrasts strikingly with his impassioned allegations. At her trial she is both eloquent and regal. Knowing that Leontes will not believe her, her speech shows courage in the face of his threat to have her killed: 'Sir, spare your threats. / The bug which you would fright me with, I seek.' She puts her faith in the judgement of the oracle.

Like Leontes, Hermione depends on Paulina. At the end of the play her only words are to Perdita: 'I, / Knowing by Paulina that the oracle / Gave hope thou wast in being, have preserved / Myself to see the issue'. Her eloquence in the first part of the play and her stillness and silence in Act 5 makes the role a very challenging one for an actor. It is impossible to say for certain whether Shakespeare expects Hermione's actions on stage to make the final reconciliation absolutely clear to the audience, or whether he leaves open the possibility of a more fragile reconciliation with Leontes.

Polixenes defies easy categorisation. In Act 1 his language is elaborate and formal. He spends much of his time resisting the encouragement of Leontes and Hermione to make him stay longer in Sicilia, then Hermione's attempts to force him to admit to mischief as a boy. Even when he is asking Camillo why Leontes seems to have changed, his imagery is elegant and detailed. In Act 4 he is concerned about the potential loss of Camillo and the behaviour of his son. His abrupt loss of temper, though he has praised Perdita's qualities, often comes as a shock to the audience and mirrors Leontes' sudden anger in Act 1.

Paulina is courageous and steadfastly loyal to Hermione. Even when Leontes threatens, 'I'll ha' thee burnt', she retorts, 'I care not'. She both comforts Leontes and reminds him of his sins, ensuring that he is not persuaded by Cleomenes and Dion into a second marriage for the good of the state. In the final scene she insists that the statue belongs to her and controls the actions and responses of those invited to view it. Paulina directs the action of much of Act 5. In Scene 1, Leontes speaks of her as his comfort and agrees never to marry until she gives him leave. She manipulates his guilt in order to achieve the resolution of the plot. In Scene 3, Paulina dominates the action by her revelation of the statue and by reminding those present that she can withdraw the statue from view. She also gives them a chance to leave if they think it is 'unlawful business / I am about'. It is Paulina who seems to bring the statue of Hermione to life and she prompts Leontes to move towards her:

> 'Tis time; descend; be stone no more; approach;
> Strike all that look upon with marvel. Come;
> I'll fill your grave up. Stir; nay, come away;
> Bequeath to death your numbness, for from him
> Dear life redeems you. You perceive she stirs.
> Start not: her actions shall be holy as
> You hear my spell is lawful. Do not shun her
> Until you see her die again, for then
> You kill her double. Nay, present your hand:
> When she was young you wooed her; now, in age,
> Is she become the suitor?   *(Act 5 Scene 3, lines 99–109)*

Paulina clearly has come to occupy an influential political position in Sicilia throughout the long period of Leontes' repentance. As page 66 shows, it was uncommon in Shakespeare's own time for a woman to become so powerful. She seems unafraid to exercise her influence, and her final speech contains a reminder to the audience that her husband, Antigonus, has been one of those who has died through Leontes' tyranny.

Camillo is seen by some to be an enigmatic character, though a Jacobean audience may have seen him as a familiar stock character: the wise and trusted counsellor. The audience becomes aware that he is a valued counsellor but it is not made clear why. It is almost as though Camillo has been like a father-confessor to Leontes:

> I have trusted thee, Camillo,
> With all the nearest things to my heart, as well
> My chamber-counsels, wherein, priest-like, thou
> Hast cleansed my bosom, I from thee departed
> Thy penitent reformed.   *(Act 1 Scene 2, lines 235–9)*

Nothing is said in the play of the guilty secrets that Leontes has confided to Camillo. Leontes also speaks of having promoted him: 'from meaner form / Have benched and reared to worship', but how or why is not explained. Camillo has been trusted with the keys to the city gates. It becomes clear in Act 4 that in the 16 years he spends in Bohemia he has risen to be Polixenes' close adviser too: 'Better not to have had thee than thus to want thee.' In some ways Camillo can be seen as a necessary function of the plot, a confidant to enable the audience to understand the motives of Leontes and Polixenes. In the escape of Perdita and Florizel too, he seems little more than an enabler.

Autolycus changes the tone of the play. When he enters singing of the change in the seasons it is as though he himself is the 'red blood' which 'reigns in the winter's pale'. He is full of vitality and openly discusses his dishonesty with the audience, making them complicit in his mischief. He is well aware of his own limitations as a coward and a petty thief. He is an engaging rogue, but Shakespeare never allows the audience to forget that he is a rogue. He receives some reward for his efforts but is finally placed in the humiliating position of having to ask the Clown for sponsorship at court (see pages 60 and 62–3 for more on Autolycus).

The **Shepherd** and the **Clown** are generous and kindly. The Shepherd's first reaction is to look after the child that he finds 'for pity'. His words have a vivid quality: 'They were warmer that got this than the poor thing is here'. His response to the finding of the gold is characteristic: ''Tis a lucky day, boy, and we'll do good deeds on't', even though the good deed turns out to be the burying of Antigonus. Jacobeans might well have recognised the Shepherd as an example of the prosperous sheep-farmers who had benefited by enclosures. The Clown is simple and easily gulled by Autolycus but Shakespeare's audience would have recognised him as a Good Samaritan figure. The audience can laugh at some of the things that the Clown says and does, but he is not entirely a figure of fun. Even when he is 'a gentleman born' he will help the man who has tricked him.

Perdita and **Florizel** are in some ways figures from the world of pastoral (see pages 61–2), the idealised shepherdess and shepherd, but they are also much more. Perdita's words link her with the changing of the seasons, the mythological figure of Proserpina, and she describes herself as 'Most goddess-like pranked up'. She is also down to earth and forthright in her rejection of Polixenes' arguments (Act 4 Scene 4, lines 99–103). Florizel is loyal and steadfast even though he thinks he is going against all convention in marrying a shepherdess. He speaks some of the most beautiful poetry in the play (Act 4 Scene 4, lines 135–46). Both Perdita and Florizel have comparatively few lines in the play but they make a lasting impression on the audience by the dramatic contrast that their open loving fidelity makes with the tortured obsession of Leontes.

Resources

Books

Dennis Bartholomeusz, *The Winter's Tale in Performance in England and America 1611–1975*, Cambridge University Press, 1982
A detailed account of the performance history of *The Winter's Tale*.

T G Bishop, *Shakespeare and the Theatre of Wonder*, Cambridge University Press, 1996
The long chapter 'The Winter's Tale; or, filling up graves' uses 'wonder' as its key to understanding the play.

Michael D Bristol, 'In Search of the Bear: Spatiotemporal Form and the Heterogeneity of Economics in *The Winter's Tale*', in S Orgel and S Keilen (eds.), *Postmodern Shakespeare*, The Critical Complex Series, Garland, 1999

Philip Brockbank (ed.), *Players of Shakespeare 1*, Cambridge University Press, 1985
Includes Gemma Jones' account of playing Hermione in a Royal Shakespeare Company production of *The Winter's Tale*.

Juliet Dusinberre, *Shakespeare and the Nature of Women*, Macmillan, second edition 1996
A feminist approach to the plays of Shakespeare and his contemporaries.

Terry Eagleton, *William Shakespeare*, Basil Blackwell, 1986
A demanding example of modern criticism that contains a brief discussion of *The Winter's Tale*.

H W Fawkner, *Shakespeare's Miracle Plays*, Associated University Presses, 1992
Argues that criticism should abandon safe ground and avoid beginning from an established critical standpoint: Christian, feminist, or other positions.

Charles Frey, *Shakespeare's Vast Romance*, University of Missouri Press, 1980
A clear summary of critical views up to date of publication. Frey's own comments on the play are in the form of an imaginary performance seen by 'we'.

Christopher Hardman, *The Winter's Tale*, Penguin Critical Studies series, Penguin, 1988
A fairly comprehensive analysis of the play. Some points seem contentious and are valuable for beginning discussions.

Frank Kermode, *Shakespeare's Language*, Allen Lane, Penguin, 2000
Stresses the variety of linguistic power displayed in *The Winter's Tale*.

F R Leavis, *The Common Pursuit*, Chatto and Windus, 1965
An example of once highly valued traditional criticism, which contains a short chapter re-evaluating the late plays.

M M Mahood, *Shakespeare's Wordplay*, Methuen, 1957
A valuable commentary on Shakespeare's use of puns and imagery.

Kenneth Muir, *Shakespeare: The Winter's Tale*, Casebook Series, Palgrave, 1968
A selection of useful extracts from criticisms of *The Winter's Tale* up to 1963.

A D Nuttall, *Studies in English Literature: The Winter's Tale*, Edward Arnold, 1966
A short but useful analysis of the play.

Bill Overton, *The Winter's Tale, The Critics' Debate*, Macmillan, 1989
An overview of major critical positions on *The Winter's Tale*.

Simon Palfrey, *Late Shakespeare: A New World of Words*, Oxford University Press, 1997
A demanding postmodern approach to the four late plays.

Robert Smallwood (ed.), *Players of Shakespeare 4*, Cambridge University Press, 1998
Includes Richard McCabe's account of playing Autolycus in a Royal Shakespeare Company production of *The Winter's Tale*.

B J Sokol, *Art and Illusion in The Winter's Tale*, Manchester University Press, 1994
A psychoanalytic approach, particularly examining Shakespeare's reference to Julio Romano.

Caroline Spurgeon, *Shakespeare's Imagery and What it Tells Us*, Cambridge University Press, 1966
First published in 1935 and now considered old-fashioned criticism but still a useful starting point for the study of Shakespeare's imagery.

E M W Tillyard, *Shakespeare's Last Plays*, Chatto and Windus, 1951
A little dated but still a useful example of a traditional critical approach.

Valerie Traub, 'Jewels, Statues and Corpses: Containment of Female Erotic Power', in S Orgel and S Keilen (eds.), *Shakespeare and Gender*, The Critical Complex Series, Garland, 1999

Derek Traversi, *Shakespeare: The Last Phase*, Hollis and Carter, 1954
A reassessment of the critical position of the late plays at the time of writing which contains useful comments on character and theme.

Roger Warren, *Staging Shakespeare's Late Plays*, Clarendon, 1990
A discussion of the ways in which productions of plays can offer new insights.

Films

The Winter's Tale has not been filmed as frequently as some of Shakespeare's other plays. Due to cost and distribution problems, only the 1981 BBC TV film and the 2001 RSC version are generally available, though others may be obtainable through libraries.

The Winter's Tale (USA, 1910) Directors: Theodore Marston and Barry O'Neil. Martin Faust (Leontes).

The Winter's Tale (UK, 1961) BBC production. Robert Shaw (Leontes), Rosalie Crutchley (Hermione).

The Winter's Tale (UK, 1968) Director: Frank Dunlop. Laurence Harvey (Leontes), Jane Asher (Perdita).

The Winter's Tale (UK, 1981) BBC production. Director: Jane Howells. Jeremy Kemp (Leontes), Anna Calder Marshal (Hermione), Robert Stephens (Polixenes).

The Winter's Tale (UK, 2001) Royal Shakespeare Company production. Director: Greg Doran. Antony Sher (Leontes), Alexandra Gilbreath (Hermione).
This is an edited version of the stage production. It includes interviews with the cast. It is also available on DVD.

Audio books

Versions available include:

Arkangel: Sinead Cusack (Hermione), Ciaran Hinds (Leontes).

HarperCollins: Peggy Ashcroft (Hermione), John Gielgud (Leontes)

Argo: Margaretta Scott (Hermione), William Squire (Leontes).

The Winter's Tale on the Web

If you type 'Winter's Tale Shakespeare' into your search engine, it will find over 56,000 items. Because websites are of wildly varying quality and rapidly disappear or are created, no recommendation can be safely made, though at the time of writing www.anglistik.uni-muenster.de/Connotations has some interesting articles. If you have time to browse, you may find much of interest.

The Winter's Tale

Sheila Innes

Series Editor: Rex Gibson

CAMBRIDGE
UNIVERSITY PRESS

PUBLISHED BY THE PRESS SYNDICATE OF THE UNIVERSITY OF CAMBRIDGE
The Pitt Building, Trumpington Street, Cambridge, United Kingdom

CAMBRIDGE UNIVERSITY PRESS
The Edinburgh Building, Cambridge CB2 2RU, UK
40 West 20th Street, New York, NY 10011–4211, USA
477 Williamstown Road, Port Melbourne, VIC 3207, Australia
Ruiz de Alarcón 13, 28014 Madrid, Spain
Dock House, The Waterfront, Cape Town 8001, South Africa

http://www.cambridge.org

First published 2002

Printed in the United Kingdom at the University Press, Cambridge

Typeface 9.5/12pt Scala   *System* QuarkXPress®

A catalogue record for this book is available from the British Library

ISBN 0 521 00817 4 paperback

Cover image: © Getty Images/PhotoDisc